What others are about this book

Walking Like Jesus is a gem. This is a primer on the practical details of living the Christian life. Whether used as a discipleship manual by new Christians or an encouragement for mature saints, this book will stimulate Christlike living. This will be a valuable tool for small group use or one-on-one mentoring.

Tedd Tripp, author of *Shepherding a Child's Heart*
Pastor, conference speaker

In a culture of life hacks and tips for greater productivity, *Walking Like Jesus* is a refreshing, countercultural call to the slow, steady way of Jesus. In it, author Larry McCall offers readers a glimpse of what it might look like to live in Christlikeness today even as we await our future glory. Pastoral and full of hope, this book will turn your eyes to the Savior.

Hannah Anderson, author of *Humble Roots: How Humility Grounds and Nourishes Your Soul*

Larry McCall has contributed a timeless treasure to the Christian world in this work. I wish every believer desiring to obey Christ could read this wonderful work. It is solidly biblical and a source of inspiration as well as instruction. I highly recommend it!

Olan Hendrix
Leadership Resource Group

This work has changed my life and continues to do so! If you have been called to a leadership role there is no greater leader to follow than the Son of God! Let me encourage you to keep this work by your desk, your bedside, and most importantly in your heart! A must-read to all in leadership roles!

Rod K. Mayer
President and Cofounder, Nextremity Solutions LLC

Written with a pastor's heart and a preacher's pen, Larry McCall helps us see the beauty of Jesus Christ and the Christlike character that the Spirit produces in the lives of his followers. Reading this book will stir fresh affections for the one who loved us and gave himself for us.

Matthew S. Harmon, Ph.D., professor of New Testament Studies, Grace College and Theological Seminary, and author of *Asking the Right Questions: A Practical Guide to Understanding and Applying the Bible*

Into a world that often asks the question "What Would Jesus Do?" and then goes on its merry way, Larry McCall leads us to look repeatedly at the more basic question: "How can we be like Jesus?" Is there a difference? You bet there is! It is character that counts, specifically the character of Jesus Christ. Actions must arise from character, to please the Lord. In chapter after chapter of this book we have the Lord Jesus displayed to us so that we can absorb and reflect his character. Larry helps us visualize the people who move across his pages, leaving us with gripping mental pictures as well as words. It is a pleasure to commend both the book and its author.

Tom Wells, author of *The Priority of Jesus Christ*

The Christian delights in Christ and longs to look more like the one they love. Yet, the path for doing so is not always clear. At times, we make it more difficult than it needs to be. Still, at other times, we treat the entire endeavor too simply. Larry McCall provides a resource for all stumbling along this path. *Walking Like Jesus* provides a careful, rich, and yet simple study for the Christian seeking to look more like their Savior. If you want to grow in Christlikeness, take a

Bible in one hand, *Walking Like Jesus* in the other, read, pray, and be prepared for the challenge and encouragement to follow after Christ even as you depend upon Christ.

Jason Helopoulos, senior pastor, University Reformed Church, East Lansing, Mich., and author of *A Neglected Grace: Family Worship in the Christian Home*

In a day of many "secrets" on how to live, we sometimes miss the obvious. Larry McCall drives us back to the foundations of Christian maturity summed up in the words, *Walk as Jesus Did*. How true! And how relevant! If we miss this, we've missed it all.

Jim Elliff, author, pastor, conference and radio speaker
President, Christian Communicators Worldwide

Becoming like Jesus Christ began growing as a passion in my life about 35 years ago. It is an immeasurable privilege to recommend Larry McCall's profound presentation of the character of our Lord. Over the years this book could have been used hundreds of times in my pastoral counseling and discipleship to point struggling people to God's perfect standard for us—Jesus Christ, his Son.

Roger Peugh, coauthor *Transformed in His Presence* and *The Need for Prayer in Counseling*

Here's a wonderful treatment of an important subject that every Christian ultimately must master. Larry McCall is uniquely qualified to write about Christian maturity and Christlikeness. I appreciate the gentleness and grace that always colors his teaching, his conversation, and his pastoral ministry. That Christlike spirit comes through in his writing, and it provides a vivid, living example that makes this an extremely powerful study.

Phillip R. Johnson, Executive Director, Grace To You

This book is Gospel-centered, doctrinally-sound, and biblically precise while also being a practical guide that truly turns one's eyes to Christ. After reading this book I have a greater love for Christ, a stronger desire to flee sin, and to be transformed into the image of Jesus. Buy this book! I can't recommend it highly enough.

Josh Mulvihill, Ph.D., GospelShapedFamily.com, author of *50 Things Every Child Needs to Know Before Leaving Home*

Walking
like Jesus

Walking
like Jesus

How to Reflect His Character Every Day

By this we may know that we are in him: whoever says he abides in him ought to walk in the same way in which he walked.
1 John 2:5–6

Dr. Larry E. McCall

Box 544
Winona Lake, IN 46590
bmhbooks.com
800-348-2756

Walking Like Jesus *How to Reflect His Character Every Day*
Copyright ©2005 by Larry E. McCall
Revised Edition 2022

Print ISBN: 978-0-88469-096-2
eBook ISBN: 978-0-88469-287-4
Printed in the United States of America

REL006710 RELIGION/Biblical Studies/New Testament/
  Jesus, the Gospels & Acts

Published by BMH Books
BMH Books
Box 544
Winona Lake, IN 46590 USA
bmhbooks.com

DEDICATION

This book is lovingly dedicated to the memory of my parents, Carl and Connie McCall, who for decades consistently reflected Christ in their everyday lives. I believe I speak not only for their children and grandchildren, but for scores of other people whose lives were impacted by their simple but profound example of Christlikeness, in saying, I thank God for them.

CONTENTS

"By this we may know that we are in him:
whoever says he abides in him
ought to walk in the same way in which he walked."
—1 John 2:5–6

ACKNOWLEDGMENTS

OVER THE DECADES, IT HAS BEEN MY DEEP JOY TO PREACH AND TEACH on the subject of walking like Jesus. Of the many people who have joined me in these life-challenging studies in the character of Christ, two in particular encouraged me to put this teaching into print. For years, they prayed for me and encouraged me to fulfill the commission of writing this book. My deep appreciation goes to my precious wife, Gladine, and to Rod Mayer, my longtime friend and spiritual accountability partner.

This book also bears the fingerprints of several gracious and competent friends who volunteered their precious time to help me sharpen and clarify the content. My thanks go to Susan Hight, Dee Woods, Don Clemens, and Steve Smilay. Lord willing, their efforts will help this book be more useful in the lives of the readers.

Terry White, the former senior editor of BMH Books, and his faithful team, encouraged me in seeing the first edition of this book come to fruition in 2005. Liz Cutler Gates, the current senior editor of BMH Books has been kind in guiding this revised edition of *Walking Like Jesus*. I count these BMH team members as friends as well as coworkers in the Lord's service.

But most of all, I thank my Lord Jesus Christ, "who loved me and gave himself for me" (Galatians 2:20). May my life, in some small way, be a reflection of his glory as I seek, by his grace, to walk as he walked. And may the Lord use this book to encourage a new generation of Christ followers to be faithful in this journey.

Larry McCall
Winona Lake, Indiana
January 2022

FOREWORD *by Jerry Bridges*

THE NEW TESTAMENT IS QUITE CLEAR THAT GOD'S ULTIMATE OBJECTIVE for all believers is conformity to the likeness of Jesus Christ. The Apostle Paul wrote in Romans 8:29 that God predestined us to be conformed to the image or likeness of his Son. Having predestined us to that end, God sets about to transform us into that image through his Spirit at work in us (2 Corinthians 3:18). Then the writer of Hebrews tells us that the purpose of God's fatherly discipline in our lives is that we may share in his holiness. That's simply another way of saying we are being conformed to his image.

The process of conforming us to the image of Jesus Christ is usually called sanctification. It is a process carried on by the Holy Spirit but involving the intentional response and cooperation of the believer. All of the moral and ethical imperatives of Scripture assume the necessity of response on our part. And it is usually to these imperatives that we who are teachers of Scripture turn when we want to address the issues of daily Christian living.

In *Walking Like Jesus*, Larry McCall reminds us of another dimension of biblical teaching that is designed to further our sanctification—the example of Jesus as he lived among the people of his day.

Sad to say, the example of Jesus' walk among us has often been overlooked or even dismissed among the evangelical sector of the Church. This has no doubt been a reaction to the message of those who deny the deity of Jesus and his substitutionary atonement for our sins but who teach that he was a good man whose example we should follow. As a result, we who rightly stress the objective work of Christ and his atoning sacrifice have tended to shy away from teaching that Jesus' life is an example for us to follow.

The Bible, however, does not do this. In the incident of washing his disciples' feet, Jesus himself said, "I have set you an example that you should do as I have done to you" (John 13:15).[1]

---

1 All Scripture quotations in this foreword are from the New International Version of the Bible.

And the apostle Peter wrote of Christ's suffering for us: "Leaving you an example, that you should follow in his steps" (1 Peter 2:21).

These two Scriptures should cast aside any doubt that we believers should pay attention to the life of Jesus so that we might follow his example.

Most of us are familiar with the WWJD slogan, "What would Jesus do?" Unfortunately, the question phrased that way opens the possibility for all kinds of subjective answers. What I think Jesus would have done in a specific situation may differ from what you think He would have done.

Pastor McCall has, in effect, helpfully rephrased that question as "What did Jesus do?" By giving us a sort of visual recording of Jesus in action in various settings, he helps us answer that question so we have concrete examples of what it means to walk like Jesus did.

One of the strengths of this book is that it takes us outside the realm of what we normally think of as Christian character. We see Jesus on a mission; and by his example, we are challenged to live purposeful lives as "people on a mission" ourselves. We see Jesus at prayer; and again, by his example, we are convicted of our own mediocre prayer lives. We see Jesus washing the feet of his disciples and learn what it means to serve others.

I have been personally challenged by this book to pay more attention to the actions of Jesus as recorded in the Gospels and to learn from them how I might more and more walk like he did. I trust this book will have a similar impact on all who read it.

Jerry Bridges (1929-2016) was a senior staff member with the Navigators for many years. He was a prolific and best-selling author. His books include The Gospel for Real Life *(2002) and* Transforming Grace *(2008) both by NavPress.*

WALKING IN THE FOOTSTEPS OF JESUS

ADAM BLEW IT. GOD, THE MASTER ARTIST, HAD CREATED HIS MASTERPIECE of the universe as a display of his glory. The focal point of this portrait was his very special creation: his image-bearers, human beings. God specially designed Adam, the first image-bearer, to reflect his Creator's glory. Adam represented God to the rest of creation and ruled this world on God's behalf.

But Adam blew it. Rather than gladly owning this wondrous life-purpose of reflecting his great Creator God, Adam selfishly succumbed to the serpent's scheme that it would be better to be God! With Adam's dreadful decision to rebel against his good Creator, sin infected the world and death invaded mankind. Adam was still God's image-bearer—still a mirror designed to reflect God— but now the mirror was cracked and muddied by sin and its effects.

Since that fateful day in the garden of Eden, we sons and daughters of Adam have been born not only in the image of our good and glorious Creator, but also in the image of our sinful and fallen ancestor, Adam. We, too, are broken mirrors, cracked by our fallenness and muddied with our sin.

So did God abandon his plan? Did he look at his rebellious image-bearers and decide to scrap his plan of filling this earth with "mirrors" designed to reflect his glory? No. God had a plan all along to send his Son as the Perfect Image-Bearer—the perfect "mirror"— into this fallen world. The Bible says this about Jesus: "He is the radiance of the glory of God and the exact imprint of his nature" (Hebrews 1:3).

That means that God's Son, Jesus Christ, is the "second Adam"— the Perfect Image-Bearer. Jesus was what the first Adam was supposed to be but wasn't. God's Son perfectly reflects his Father's glory, a mirror with no cracks of fallenness, no mud of sin.

But where does that leave us? Is there any hope for us broken mirrors? Does God have a plan to restore us to be the mirrors he designed us to be? That's what this book is about. What is God's plan for those of us who have placed our faith in Jesus? How is God transforming us to be more and more like Jesus, the Perfect Image-Bearer?

This book is a humble attempt to help those who claim to be Christians better understand what it means to "walk like Jesus." Mirroring the character of Jesus should be the normal pattern of life for the Christian as he or she goes about everyday life at work, at school, in the neighborhood, at church, and at home.

In these chapters we will focus on certain character traits Jesus demonstrated during his earthly ministry. We will also explore explicit biblical commands to daily mirror those character traits of Jesus and to understand how God's Holy Spirit graciously transforms us to reflect Christ.

My heartfelt desire is that readers don't lay down this book and say, "That was nice." Instead, my hope and prayer is that each one will finish reading and say, "Lord, change me! Mold me to increasingly reflect Jesus so that I can impact my family, my church, and my community for your glory and their good!"

I pray we will gradually, but surely, be conformed to Christ as the Holy Spirit takes the teaching of the Word of God and applies it to our lives. The apostle Paul wrote, "We all, with unveiled face, beholding the glory of the Lord, are being transformed into the same image from one degree of glory to another. For this comes from the Lord who is the Spirit" (2 Corinthians 3:18).

> My dear Redeemer and my Lord,
> I read my duty in thy Word;
> But in thy life the law appears
> Drawn out in living characters.
> Such was thy truth, and such thy zeal,
> Such deference to thy Father's will,
> Such love, and meekness so divine,
> I would transcribe and make them mine.

Be thou my pattern; make me bear
More of thy gracious image here:
Then God the Judge shall own my name
Amongst the followers of the Lamb.

—Isaac Watts

Discussion Questions
WALKING IN THE FOOTSTEPS OF JESUS

1. In your own words, define the word *Christian*.

2. According to 1 John 2, how important is it that the daily conduct of professing Christians match their *claim* of being a follower of Christ?

3. What are some potential dangers of assuring people of their salvation based only on their claim?

4. What are some character traits of Jesus that you would especially like to see better mirrored in your own life as a result of this study?

5. Spend time praying for the Holy Spirit to work in your life to better display those character traits.

Chapter 1

WHY WALK LIKE JESUS?

WHO IS THE MOST FAMOUS PERSON EVER? TRY DOING A SEARCH ONLINE. I did. Want to guess who was number 1 on every website I found on that issue? You guessed it: Jesus Christ of Nazareth. Jesus has captivated the attention of billions of people over the centuries.

Many of us profess to be his followers. Being a follower of Jesus implies having some understanding of where he is going and being committed to following him there. His commitments become our commitments. His character becomes ours. The Apostle John said it like this: "Whoever says he abides in him ought to walk in the same way in which he walked" (1 John 2:6). How well do we know this Jesus we are professing to follow? How clearly do we understand his character traits that God calls us to reflect? And how does that happen in real life?

In this book we are going on a quest together. Our quest is to see Jesus more clearly. And, by God's grace, we will find hope and help in our commitment to pursue Christlikeness in our lives—to walk as Jesus did.

Reasons for Our Quest

Going on this quest of pursuing Christ and Christlikeness is a significant lifelong commitment. Why devote ourselves to such a big endeavor? A study of the New Testament reveals five reasons:

1. *Christlikeness is our passion.* When we are drawn to Christ in salvation, we find that he becomes precious to us. The more we get to know him, the more we want to know him. Then, knowing him more and more leads to becoming more like our Savior every day.

After decades of being a Christian, the imprisoned missionary, Paul, could still write with passion, "I want to know Christ" (Philippians 3:10 NIV).

Early twentieth-century gospel songwriter Charles H. Gabriel wrote, "More like the Master I would ever be." If you love him, doesn't your heart resonate with those words?

When Christ becomes our Savior, the Holy Spirit gives us a love for Jesus that moves us to want to know him better and reflect him in our lives.

2. *Christlikeness is our calling.* Jesus stood before a Galilean crowd and said, "Come to me, all who labor and are heavy laden, and I will give you rest. Take my yoke upon you, and *learn from me*, for I am gentle and lowly in heart, and you will find rest for your souls. For my yoke is easy, and my burden is light" (Matthew 11:28–30). For his followers, Jesus is King. And King Jesus himself has given us his gracious command to come to him to learn—to learn who God is, who we are, how we can be right with God, and how we can live for his glory.

We are not called primarily to an institution or a particular body of doctrine but to a real Person. It is from that real Person, with all his marvelous attributes, that we are to learn about life and eternity. King Jesus commands it, and we must obey his call. As we respond, our initiation into Christ must be followed by our imitation of Christ.

3. *Christlikeness is our obligation.* Professing that we are connected to Christ in salvation carries with it an obligation to back up that claim with a lifestyle that mirrors the character of Christ. This is at the heart of John's statement, "By this we may know that we are in him: whoever says he abides in him ought to walk in the same way in which he walked" (1 John 2:5–6). Faith in Jesus as our Savior and conformity to his character are inseparable.

Being like Christ is the standard for Christians. Theologian and pastor Sinclair Ferguson writes, "In a word, maturity equals Christlikeness. No other standard may be allowed to substitute. All other standards will be lesser, man-made alternatives that disguise the all-demanding standard God sets before us in the Scriptures."[1]

Repeatedly in the New Testament, we Christians are called upon to follow Christ in our paths to Christian maturity. In addition to 1 John 2:5–6, consider these calls to Christlikeness:

- Jesus said, "I have given you an example, that you also should do just as I have done to you" (John 13:15).

- The apostle Paul wrote, "Your attitude should be the same as that of Christ Jesus" (Philippians 2:5 NIV).

- The apostle Peter wrote, "Christ also suffered for you, leaving you an example, so that you should follow in his steps" (1 Peter 2:21).

If we are not seeking to reflect the character of Christ in our lives, what right do we have to claim to be Christians?

4. *Christlikeness is our best witness.* Much of what the watching world knows of Jesus Christ comes from observing the lifestyles of those who claim to be united to Christ. The world's opinions of Christ largely reflect the world's opinions of Christ's followers.

It's helpful to remember that the early Christians were living in a culture that, for the most part, did not yet have the New Testament. What the non-Christians knew of Christ they gleaned not only from what they heard from those early Christians but from what they saw in them. When believers in the first century lived everyday life in a Christ-reflecting way, the non-Christians around them could see the powerful effectiveness of God's extraordinary gospel in the lives of ordinary people, such as their Christian relatives, coworkers, and neighbors.

Perhaps that's the implication of the apostle Paul's choice of words to the early believers on Crete to "make the teaching about God our Savior attractive" (Titus 2:10 NIV).

Our own culture has been marked by a growing biblical illiteracy. As a result, our era increasingly mirrors the first century's lack of knowledge regarding the New Testament Scriptures. Once again, much of what the watching world knows of Christ is gained from observing the everyday lives of Christians around them.

Today's Christians have the opportunity not only to speak the gospel message (which we must) but also to demonstrate visually the life-changing effectiveness of the gospel through the ways we reflect Christ. On the other hand, nothing will weaken our witness more than a wide gap between what we say and how we live. The watching world will quickly turn away in disinterest, if not disdain, when they perceive hypocrisy.

5. *Christlikeness is our destiny.* As much as it might feel like it at times, our lives are not going in circles! As Christians, we are heading for a destiny that God had planned for us even before he said, "Let there be light." Paul wrote of this destiny in Romans 8. Many Christians find great comfort in quoting Romans 8:28: "We know that for those who love God all things work together for good, for those who are called according to his purpose."

However, I suspect few believers have explored that passage to discover what Paul was referring to as "the good" that God is working in our lives. The next words from Paul's pen explain that our preplanned destination is "to be conformed to the image of his Son" (v. 29).

Why would God plan such a glorious destiny for us?

To better appreciate the significance of our God-ordained destiny, go back to the beginning of the human race. God decided to make one of his creations special. He said he would make human beings in his "likeness." And they would rule over all other created things on behalf of God, the Great King. (See Genesis 1:26.)

God created Adam and Eve in his own image in order to reflect him, represent him, and rule for him as his "prince and princess." Yet the prince and princess rebelled against the Great King, desiring to be their own bosses rather than to serve as their Sovereign's representative. Because of their rebellion, sin tarnished God's likeness in human beings. And we have not fulfilled our designed role ever since.

Significantly, the job description of every person as God's image bearers is still in force but unfulfilled. The author of Hebrews says that God has crowned him with glory and honor, putting everything in subjection under his feet" (Hebrews 2:6–8).

Then the author adds the sad reality that presently we don't see everything subject to us.

We might despair were it not for the encouraging words that follow, "But we see him who for a little while was made lower than the angels, namely Jesus, crowned with glory and honor because of the suffering of death, so that by the grace of God he might taste death for everyone" (v. 9).

In other words, the first Adam did not fulfill his obligations as God's image bearer. However, God never abandoned his goal of having us operate as his special representatives, ruling in the name of the Great King. When the first Adam failed in his mission, God set in motion his plan of redemption and restoration. He sent his own perfect Son in real human flesh as the "last Adam" to restore what was lost by the sin of the first image bearer. (See 1 Corinthians 15:45.)

God's School of Redemption

Now, as the great goal of our redemption, God is bringing all things into our lives for "the good" of making us like Christ. He is shaping us, conforming us to Jesus' likeness. We are currently in God's school of redemption, becoming more and more like Jesus. That's God's ultimate goal in our sanctification—to make us more and more like his Son Jesus, who is the Perfect Image-Bearer. (See Hebrews 1:3.)

John Stott wrote, "God's whole purpose, conceived in a past eternity, being worked out for and in his people in history, to be completed in the glory to come, may be encapsulated in this single concept: God intends to make us like Christ."[2]

Right now, in God's school of redemption, we may feel as if we still have so much to learn, so much that yet needs to change in us. But graduation day awaits! "We know that when he appears we shall be like him, because we shall see him as he is" (1 John 3:2). And then, having been conformed into the image of Jesus, the "last Adam," we shall "reign forever and ever" in his likeness and under his perfect leadership (Revelation 22:5). This is our preplanned destination. If he is currently bringing all things into our lives to work that "good" in us, then our classwork includes knowing all we can about our Savior. He is the One into whose image we are being restored. It is our destiny to be like Jesus.

Why desire to be like Jesus? That is our passion, our calling, our obligation, our best witness, and ultimately, our destiny. Above all, reflecting Christ's character is our high privilege.

God calls us to devote ourselves to the study of Christ through his holy Word, praying that his Holy Spirit would conform us more and more to the image of our blessed Savior.

May the mind of Christ my Savior,
Live in me from day to day,
By His love and power controlling
All I do and say.
May the love of Jesus fill me,
As the waters fill the sea;
Him exalting, self abasing,
This is victory.

—Kate B. Wilkinson

Discussion Questions

WHY WALK LIKE JESUS?

1. Name several reasons for desiring to be like Christ.

2. Which one of these reasons especially captures your interest? Why?

3. Briefly tell about a person who "preached with his or her life." What kind of impact did that example make on you?

4. Finish this sentence: "God intends to make us ...."

5. Thus far in your Christian experience, what has Christian maturity looked like? How do you think this picture might change through a study of Christlikeness?

6. Spend time praying, asking God to continue his work of making you more like Jesus—no matter what that might take.

Chapter 2

WALKING IN MEEKNESS LIKE JESUS

WHAT A SIGHT IT MUST HAVE BEEN! A PARADE OF FOREIGNERS WAS PASSING through the streets of Jerusalem—Gentiles from the east. This entourage of foreign-looking, foreign-sounding men were looking for a king, and they asked the local folks for directions to the king's palace.

But when they finally arrived there, they found no baby king. Instead, King Herod's advisors told these magi to look in the nearby village of Bethlehem.

There, in that small, humble town, they found the young King they were seeking, the King who had been born in a stable.

I think we are so familiar with the story of Jesus' birth and the wise men's visit that we often miss a significant incongruity. How strange it was that the King of kings would be born, not in a king's palace but in a stable designed for horses, donkeys, and camels. Why would the King of kings choose to make his entrance in such a humble setting?

In the previous chapter of this book, we learned of Jesus' gracious call to come "learn from me" (Matthew 11:29). He continued, "for I am gentle and lowly in heart." That word *gentle* can also be translated, "humble" or "meek."

Jesus invites us—actually commands us—to come learn from him, the One who describes himself as "meek and lowly in heart" (KJV).

This is such a loving invitation. How do we learn meekness from Jesus Christ?

What is Meekness?

Various dictionary definitions of the English word *meek* convey the ideas of being mild, not violent, not easily angered or resentful—even submissive. Some people draw a slight distinction between humility and meekness: Humility is an attitude or attribute people have within themselves. Meekness is the way a humble person relates to others.

In our western culture, *meekness* sometimes carries a negative connotation of powerlessness or weakness. This distortion doesn't fit Jesus Christ, does it? He characterized himself as meek, yet he certainly was not weak or powerless. In fact, Jesus said he was greater than Abraham. Christ demonstrated his lordship over sickness, demons, death—even sin. We can't afford to let modern distortions determine our understanding of the biblical concept of meekness.

In the Bible, meekness is the demeanor of people who accept the place God has appointed for them. Meek people embrace the role God has ordained for them individually.

Ultimately, we learn the meaning of meekness, not from dictionaries or from popular concepts but by observing the One who is the benchmark of meekness. Jesus is the epitome, the defining standard, the very embodiment of meekness.

1. *Jesus was meek in his attitudes.* Philippians 2:5–6 says, "Your attitude should be the same as that of Christ Jesus: who being in very nature God, did not consider equality with God something to be grasped" (NIV).

It is important to remember that Jesus Christ had existed from all eternity past as God. He had enjoyed all the indescribable glories of heaven (John 17:5). Yet, as he walked on this earth, he did not assert that role or demand that glory. He never used his "God-ness" as a means of self-promotion or self-protection. Out of love for us, his people, he chose not to cling to the privileges rightfully his. He willingly waived his rights in order to serve others.

Jesus did not pull rank. Instead, he humbled himself and chose to "be made like his brothers in every respect, so that he might become a merciful and faithful high priest in the service of God, to make propitiation for the sins of the people" (Hebrews 2:17).

2. *Jesus was meek in his actions.* Paul wrote that Jesus "emptied himself, by taking the form of a servant, being born in the likeness of men. And being found in human form, he humbled himself by becoming obedient to the point of death, even death on a cross" (Philippians 2:7–8). The Prince of Glory "stepped down" to become the Son of Man.

Stepping Down

When God the Son came to this fallen planet, he laid aside the independent use of his divine prerogatives.

1. *Jesus stepped down from heaven to earth.* From the moment he created the heavenly beings, Jesus had heard the continual praise of "Holy, Holy, Holy." Yet the first sounds he heard in that birthing stable were the grating sounds of donkeys and camels. He who had smelled the heavenly incense was now subject to the odors of urine-soaked straw, animal manure, and human sweat.

The One who had been rich beyond measure became poor for us. Paul wrote, "You know the grace of our Lord Jesus Christ, that though he was rich, yet for your sake he became poor, so that you by his poverty might become rich" (2 Corinthians 8:9). He who had been the Lawgiver humbled himself to become a "Lawkeeper." The apostle Paul put it this way: "When the fullness of time had come, God sent forth his Son, born of woman, born under the law" (Galatians 4:4).

Author Les Carter writes, "Can you grasp the enormity of this event in the manger? Only a face-to-face meeting with the Lamb in heaven will let us truly appreciate his incarnation. When we see Jesus robed in the glory that was rightfully his, we will be truly awed at his willingness to embrace humanity in this way, and we will understand that his greatness is anchored in the unlikely characteristic of humility."[3]

2. *Jesus stepped down from glory to humility.* From the moment he left heaven's throne to the moment he rose from the grave, Jesus lived a life, not of glory but of humility. The Creator God walked on the very planet he personally had spoken into existence. Yet "the world

15

did not know him. He came to his own, and his own people did not receive him" (John 1:10–11). Vainly we try to imagine the humiliation of the King of kings walking down a crowded road and being recognized by no one. No one cared. Jesus was continually misunderstood, rejected, and persecuted.

3. *Jesus stepped down from master to servant.* The King of kings became a servant of sinners. During those silent years from early childhood to age thirty, Jesus lived a humble life. In childhood he submitted himself to his earthly parents (Luke 2:51), even though he was their Lord. He humbled himself to live in a home with sinful parents and half-siblings. He worked a normal blue-collar job as a contractor, building and fixing things for people in his Nazareth neighborhood. Nobody in the village recognized him as anything special. When he preached his first public sermon, his neighbors reacted with "Is not this Joseph's son?" (Luke 4:22). In fact, Matthew adds, "They took offense at him" (Matthew 13:57). Truly, meekness marked Jesus' first thirty years on earth.

Then, in his public ministry, he demonstrated meekness as a lifestyle. With whom did he associate? Whom did he serve? Jesus befriended and ministered to fishermen, tax collectors, beggars, lepers, prostitutes, gentiles, and other foreigners.

How different the meek Jesus was from the proud, pompous Pharisees, who distanced themselves from these outcasts of Jewish society! Jesus was a friend of sinners.

As he carried out his public ministry, the Bread of Life became hungry, the Water of Life became thirsty, and the Creator of the Universe had "nowhere to lay his head" (Matthew 8:20). Even in his supposed moment of glory on Palm Sunday, people said of Jesus (quoting Zechariah 9:9), "Behold, your king is coming to you, humble [or meek], and mounted on a donkey" (Matthew 21:5, brackets added). Jesus himself testified to his meekness when he told his followers, "The Son of Man came not to be served but to serve, and to give his life as a ransom for many" (Matthew 20:28).

4. *Jesus stepped down from life to death.* As the ultimate act of meekness, the Son of God stepped down from life to death. The One who was identified as "the Author of life" (Acts 3:15) voluntarily

submitted to death at the hands of wicked men. The One who had life in himself voluntarily laid aside his own life so he could die for unworthy sinners. He willingly died a painful, shameful death. "He humbled himself by becoming obedient to the point of death, even death on a cross" (Philippians 2:8).

The Impact of Christ's Meekness on Us

One way we can mirror Christ's meekness is through our attitudes. In Philippians 2:5, the apostle Paul urges us to adopt the same mindset that Christ had. And when we are secure in our relationship with the Father through Jesus Christ, we increasingly grasp the reality that God is God and we are not. The foundation for Christlike meekness, Paul says, is our undeserved union with Jesus, his comforting love, and our fellowship with the Spirit. (See Philippians 2:1.) If we understand that our relationship with God the Father is based entirely on grace, there is no room for pride and no need for self-promotion or self-defense. That's the impact of Jesus' meekness in us.[4]

What about our relationships with other people? Meekness is humility that considers others better than ourselves (Philippians 2:3).

- Meekness means promoting others, not promoting ourselves. (One indicator of a lack of meekness is expending emotional energy to avoid our own humiliation.)

- Meekness means pursuing unity in our families and our churches. Pride promotes our own preferences and agendas. But meekness, in sensitivity, adapts to the needs and preferences of others. We can work well with other believers, "by being of the same mind, having the same love, being in full accord and of one mind" (Philippians 2:2).

Another way to mirror Christ's meekness is through our actions. Jesus described himself as "meek and lowly in heart" (Matthew 11:29 KJV). And he demonstrated that in the way he served others—even if it required personal sacrifice.

- Meekness means pursuing the interests of others instead of letting our selfish ambition rule our actions.

- Meekness means caring for the welfare of others—especially our brothers and sisters in Christ.
- Meekness means developing a lifestyle of helping others. When we see a need, we look for ways to help—and we follow through.
- Meekness means willingly serving others—even when it's inconvenient or we have to sacrifice something to do it.

Jesus Christ's meekness permeated his attitudes and his actions. He has graciously commanded us to come learn from him because he is "meek and lowly of heart." As we contemplate our Savior and Teacher, we will be "transformed into his [meek] likeness" (2 Corinthians 3:18 NIV).

South African pastor Andrew Murray wrote, "A proud follower of the humble Jesus—this I cannot, I may not be."[5] Lord, do your refining work. Make us more like our meek Savior.

> "Man of Sorrows!" what a name
> For the Son of God, who came
> Ruined sinners to reclaim!
> Hallelujah! what a Savior!
> Bearing shame and scoffing rude,
> In my place condemned he stood;
> Sealed my pardon with his blood;
> Hallelujah! what a Savior!
>
> —Philip P. Bliss

Discussion Questions

WALKING IN MEEKNESS LIKE JESUS

1. Begin by prayerfully reading Philippians 2:1–11 several times.

2. How would you define the word *meek*?

3. Give some examples of ways Jesus showed meekness in his attitudes.

4. Give some examples of ways Jesus showed meekness in his actions. Can you think of some stories in the Bible that illustrate this?

5. How does being "meek like Jesus" relate to the popular notion of building self-esteem?

6. What are some ways you could show meekness to those closest to you (family, friends, fellow church members)?

7. How should the meekness of Jesus affect the corporate life of the church?

Chapter 3
WALKING "ON MISSION" LIKE JESUS

ON A SPRING DAY IN THE MIDDLE EAST, A PARADE OF PEOPLE WALKED along the palm-tree-lined streets of the picturesque valley town of Jericho. The week before the Passover, travelers always passed through Jericho as they journeyed toward the mountaintop city of Jerusalem for the festival. Yet on this memorable day, one traveler drew the attention of everyone. In fact, crowds of locals gathered along the route to get a glimpse of the prominent man and his entourage.

They wanted to see the young rabbi whose extraordinary preaching and astounding miracles had gained him significant renown. No doubt, many Jericho citizens wondered if this young rabbi and his followers would stay overnight in their beautiful city to rest before the arduous climb from the deep Jordan Valley to Jerusalem. Would the young preacher stay in the home of one of the local priests or rabbis? That seemed appropriate.

As people jostled positions for a good look at this rabbi everyone had been talking about, a nicely dressed short man was finding it difficult to get a good vantage point for viewing Jesus and his followers. No one in the crowd let this wealthy man pass through to the front. No one moved aside for Zacchaeus. Why should they? He was a tax collector—one of the most detested jobs imaginable to the Jews.

But this was no run-of-the-mill tax collector. Zacchaeus was a chief tax collector. He oversaw their whole district, one of only three chief tax collectors in all of Palestine.

Zacchaeus was doubly unpopular with his Jericho neighbors. Not only did he line his own pockets at the expense of his fellow Jews; he also worked for the hated gentile occupiers, the Romans. Imagine, a Jew getting rich by fleecing his fellow Jews in the name of the Roman government. No wonder no one wanted to let this curious, contemptable, short man have a front-row seat to see Jesus.

Zacchaeus, however, an enterprising man, came up with a novel solution. He climbed one of the sycamore-fig trees growing near the street. What a sight that must have been! One of the most notorious, filthy-rich citizens of Jericho was climbing a tree like a schoolboy.

Soon the crowds saw Jesus approaching. They craned their necks to get a better look. He appeared ordinary, but the stories about him were far from it. Many common people found him fascinating. He preached in ways they understood. He was so kind. He showed compassion to ordinary, lowly people—just like them.

The religious leaders, though, resented Jesus immensely. Rumors spread that something was going to happen during the Passover. Would the religious establishment confront the miracle worker from Galilee? Who would get the upper hand?

As the citizens of Jericho watched and wondered, Jesus suddenly stopped under Zacchaeus's sycamore-fig tree. Can you picture the cynical smiles spreading across the faces in the crowd? Many may have watched with joyful anticipation. Maybe the rabbi from Galilee would put this wealthy traitor in his place. Maybe Jesus would rebuke him in front of all these people Zacchaeus had robbed.

Surely Zacchaeus was flabbergasted when he realized that the parade had stopped directly under his tree.

Jesus' Mission on Display

Suddenly Jesus looked up and said, "Zacchaeus, hurry and come down, for I must stay at your house today" (Luke 19:5).

What? Did Jesus say he was going to stay in the home of that sinner? Why would he do such a thing? The crowd surely wondered.

Jesus' words indicated that he saw their meeting as a divine appointment. Literally, Jesus said, "It is necessary for me to stay at your house today." Not merely out on a casual afternoon stroll, Jesus came there on a divine mission. He had a purpose in going to the house of this corrupt businessman. Although Zacchaeus was glad to be part of this divine appointment, the crowds voiced their displeasure. "He has gone in to be the guest of a man who is a sinner," they grumbled (Luke 19:7).

But Jesus knew his mission so clearly that the irate crowd did not dissuade him.

As we follow Jesus and Zacchaeus to the tax collector's Jericho villa, we find an astonishing scene. Zacchaeus has become a transformed man. He who previously had been greedy and dishonest in his business dealings is now humble and repentant. He says, "Behold, Lord, the half of my goods I give to the poor. And if I have defrauded anyone of anything, I restore it fourfold " (Luke 19:8). How could anyone explain this amazing change?

Jesus announced to everyone there, "Today salvation has come to this house." We can't explain the change in Zacchaeus in human terms. It is a miracle. Such a change comes about only by the intervention of saving grace.

Before Jesus leaves Zacchaeus's home to finish his journey to Jerusalem—and the crucifixion that awaits him—he clearly declares his purpose statement, his mission. He says to the grateful Zacchaeus and to the grumbling neighbors, "The Son of Man came to seek and to save the lost" (Luke 19:10).

Jesus' Mission Declared

The unforgettable dinner at Zacchaeus's house was not the only time Jesus declared his mission statement. Over and over, both he and others said he came to this sin-filled earth as a Man on a mission. Jesus' purpose shaped his whole life.

- Even before Jesus was born in Bethlehem, the angel announced his mission. The angel said, "You shall call his name Jesus, for he will save his people from their sins" (Matthew 1:21).

- Early in Jesus' life he asked his mother and stepfather, "Did you not know that I must be in my Father's house?" (Luke 2:49).

- As he began his public ministry, he revealed his awareness of his purpose on earth. "I have come to…fulfill the Law and Prophets" (Matthew 5:17 NIV).

- He also said, "My food is to do the will of him who sent me and to accomplish his work" (John 4:34).

- Later in his ministry, he explained to his disciples, "The Son of Man came not to be served but to serve, and to give his life as a ransom for many" (Matthew 20:28).

- Matthew recalled this about the latter part of Jesus' ministry: "From that time Jesus began to show his disciples that he must go to Jerusalem" (Matthew 16:21).

- As he went through the Passion Week, Jesus told them, "Now is my soul troubled. And what shall I say? 'Father, save me from this hour'? But for this purpose I have come to this hour. Father, glorify your name" (John 12:27–28).

- As he stood before Pilate, Jesus reiterated, "For this purpose I was born and for this purpose I have come into the world—to bear witness to the truth" (John 18:37).

- And Jesus' proclaimed his ultimate mission in that triumphant cry from the cross, "It is finished!" (John 19:30). Mission accomplished!

Jesus came to do the will of his Father. He came to seek and to save those who were lost. He came to glorify his Father's name. *And he did it!* He completed the work the Father had given him (John 17:4).

After Jesus went back to heaven, the Holy Spirit reminded the apostles of Jesus' mission. For example, Paul would later teach, "God sent forth his Son…to redeem those who were under the law" (Galatians 4:4–5). And the author of Hebrews wrote, "Therefore he had to be made like his brothers in every respect, so that he might become a merciful and faithful high priest in the service of God, to make propitiation for the sins of the people" (Hebrews 2:17).

The words of Jesus, and his apostles, repeatedly teach us that he was a Man on a mission. There was nothing haphazard about his life and ministry. He did everything for one goal: to accomplish that purpose. Hebrews says that when Christ came, he said, "I have come to do your will, O God" (10:7). In doing so, Jesus brought his Father glory (John 17:4).

When we look at the life and character of Jesus, we see him focused on his purpose of seeking and saving what was lost. We truly see him as a Man on a mission—determined to glorify the Father by doing his will.

Jesus' Mission Replicated in His Apostles

As Jesus prepared for his physical departure from the earth, thoughts of "passing the missions baton to his apostles" filled his mind.

Talking to his heavenly Father the night before his crucifixion, Jesus prayed, "As you sent me into the world, so I have sent them into the world" (John 17:18).

Several days later, on the evening of Resurrection Sunday, Jesus appeared to his disciples and announced, "As the Father has sent me, even so I am sending you" (John 20:21).

And what were Jesus' last words as he ascended into heaven? "You will receive power when the Holy Spirit has come upon you, and you will be my witnesses in Jerusalem and in all Judea and Samaria, and to the end of the earth" (Acts 1:8).

How did Christ's mission-mindedness affect the lives and ministries of his apostles?

Paul, for example, became totally wrapped up in carrying on Jesus' mission. He wrote, "We are ambassadors for Christ, God making his appeal through us. We implore you on behalf of Christ, be reconciled to God" (2 Corinthians 5:20).

Paul couldn't stop telling people the good news of salvation in Jesus Christ. He told the believers in Corinth that he had endured multiple imprisonments, countless beatings, several stonings, was shipwrecked three times, and lived with constant danger and hardship (2 Corinthians 11:24–28. What kept Paul going? Why didn't he just quit? He explained his life purpose this way: "I am compelled to preach. Woe to me if I do not preach the gospel!" (1 Corinthians 9:16 NIV).

Jesus' Mission Replicated in Us

What does it mean to be people on a mission, to mirror our Lord and Savior? As followers of Jesus Christ, we have eternal purpose.

Meandering through life is not an option. Haphazard living is not an option. Living to please ourselves with whatever captures our interest at the time is not an option. God calls us to commit ourselves to being people on a mission.

Based on his ultimate authority, Jesus himself commissioned us: "Go therefore and make disciples of all nations, baptizing them in the name of the Father and of the Son and of the Holy Spirit, teaching them to observe all that I have commanded you." And then he promised, "Behold, I am with you always, to the end of the age" (Matthew 28:18–20).

The apostle Peter explained our mission this way: "Proclaim the excellencies of him who called you out of darkness into his marvelous light" (1 Peter 2:9–10). This is purposeful living: carrying out our assigned mission, telling the world the glorious gospel of our Savior.

Often, when we hear the word *missions*, our minds automatically default to thoughts of a small, select band of people who are called to take the gospel to faraway, exotic lands. While we are thankful for and support those cross-cultural missionaries, our Lord wants us to look for everyday opportunities to carry out the mission he gave us. We have the privilege to "proclaim the excellencies of him who called you [us] out of darkness into his marvelous light" in our daily encounters with people around us.

We can mirror Jesus' mission as we go to our schools and workplaces, each day. As we increasingly reflect the character of our Lord Jesus, nonbelievers around us may grow curious. By the way we live, we can give them reasons for asking what makes us different from our classmates or coworkers. The apostle Peter wrote, "In your hearts honor Christ the Lord as holy, always being prepared to make a defense to anyone who asks you for a reason for the hope that is in you; yet do it with gentleness and respect" (1 Peter 3:15).

We can mirror Jesus' mission as we live in our communities. Praying to have the eyes and heart of Jesus more consistently, we will begin to see people as individuals who need to hear the good news about salvation in Christ alone.

We can mirror Jesus' mission as we reflect more brightly our Lord's character to unsaved family members. With "gentleness and respect" (1 Peter 3:15), we speak warmly of our Savior, praying that he will open the eyes of our family members, even as he did ours.

Ultimately, Jesus came to do the will of his Father. He came to seek and to save those who were lost. He came to glorify his Father's name. *And he did it!* He completed the work the Father had given him (John 17:4). And he calls us to do the same.

O for a thousand tongues to sing
My great Redeemer's praise,
The glories of my God and King,
The triumphs of His grace.
My gracious Master and my God,
Assist me to proclaim,
To spread through all the earth abroad
The honors of Thy Name.

—Charles Wesley

Discussion Questions

WALKING "ON MISSION" LIKE JESUS

1. From Luke 19:10, write out Jesus' mission statement.

2. Did Jesus devise his own mission statement, or was it assigned to him? (Read Matthew 1:21 and John 17:4.)

3. How aware was Jesus of his mission as he lived here on earth? (Read Luke 2:49–50; Luke 4:16–21; John 4:34; Matthew 16:21–23; John 19:30.)

4. How did Jesus' awareness of his mission affect him? (Read John 12:23–28; Matthew 26:36–42; John 18:36–37.)

5. Where do we Christians get our life's mission statement? Is it one that we have come up with ourselves, or has it been assigned to us? (Read John 20:21 and Matthew 28:18–20.)

6. On a slip of paper, write the names of three people you would like to talk to about Jesus. Use that slip of paper as a bookmark for your daily Bible reading, reminding you to pray for opportunities to witness to those three people.

Chapter 4
LIVING INCARNATIONALLY LIKE JESUS

HE WAS SO TIRED. WHAT AN EXHAUSTING DAY! HE HAD PREACHED MUL-tiple times, and now he had to deal with the pressure of the crowds. He climbed into the back of the boat, made a makeshift bed out of a cushion, and soon fell into a deep sleep. So deep, in fact, that he didn't stir even when the boat began pitching and tossing. Water poured from the sky and gushed over the boat's gunwales. And on he slept.

The situation became more and more desperate. The wild-eyed disciples shook Jesus out of his much-needed sleep. "Lord, save us! We're going to drown!" they shouted above the storm.

Can you see Jesus pushing the rain-soaked hair out of his eyes and turning toward the panicked voices?

He shook off the deep sleep and crawled off his drenched cushion. Bracing himself, he stood up in the back of that tossing boat. No doubt sounding a bit like an exhausted dog owner at the back door of his house in the middle of the night, Jesus shouted to the wind and waves, "Quiet! Be still!" The wind and the waves, like that misbehaving dog, knew the voice of their Master and immediately calmed down at his command.

The writers of the Gospels don't tell us whether Jesus went back to sleep. I would not be surprised if he did. But they do tell us about his companions. Matthew recalled that unforgettable night and tells us they were all amazed. "What sort of man is this, that even the winds and sea obey him?" they asked. (Matthew 8:27).

Indeed. What kind of man is this? Into what category does someone like Jesus fit? What kind of man can at one moment lie in exhausted sleep and at the next moment command the wind and the waves to be quiet?

What kind of man is this? To find the answer, we go back to the beginning. Not merely to the beginning of Jesus' ministry. Not merely to the beginning of his life here on earth. Not merely to the beginning of time. Even before that. We sweep back the curtain of time and peer into eternity past.

John 1:1–3 invites us to a time before God created the universe. "In the beginning was the Word." The context tells us the Word refers to Jesus. "And the Word was with God, and the Word was God. He was in the beginning with God. All things were made through him, and without him was not any thing made that was made." Then the Gospel writer astonishes us with these words: "The Word became flesh and dwelt among us, and we have seen his glory, glory as of the only Son from the Father, full of grace and truth" (John 1:14).

Did you catch that intriguing title of Jesus: "the only Son"? The word *only* in this context means "unique." Jesus is the only one of his kind, the only one in his category. That's why those storm-drenched disciples were so baffled. Jesus defied categorization. They asked in bewilderment, "What *kind* of man is this?" They couldn't place Jesus into any category because He is the *only* One of his kind. Jesus *alone* is both God and man. Jesus is God in the flesh. We use the word *incarnate* to describe this incredible truth.

What Jesus Had Always Been

The Bible teaches that Jesus had always existed in eternity past. "In the beginning was the Word" (John 1:1). Again, *the Word,* here, is Jesus. Have you ever wondered what life was like for Jesus before he came to the earth? Think about these truths from John 1:1–3:

1. *Jesus had always existed in eternity past*—with *God.* "The Word was with God." We can only try to imagine the eternal, perfect relationship of love between God the Father and God the Son.

What might we learn from this phrase in Jesus's prayer? "You loved me before the foundation of the world" (John 17:24). Think about that eternal Father-Son relationship. No sin. No hatred. No rejection. Not even fear of rejection. Only perfect, eternal love.

2. *Jesus had always existed in eternity past*—as *God.* "The Word was God." The astonishing reality is that the pre-Bethlehem Jesus was the absolute owner of the universe! That's what Psalm 50 refers to: "Every beast of the forest is mine, the cattle on a thousand hills. I know all the birds of the hills, and all that moves in the field is mine…the world and its fullness are mine" (vv. 10–12).

And have you ever read Isaiah 6:1–3 and found your heart stirred? It's mind-boggling, isn't it?

This is Isaiah's testimony of his vision: "I saw the Lord sitting upon a throne, high and lifted up; and the train of his robe filled the temple. Above him stood the seraphim. Each had six wings: with two he covered his face, and with two he covered his feet, and with two he flew. And one called to another and said: "Holy, holy, holy is the Lord of hosts; the whole earth is full of his glory!'" The apostle John opens our eyes to an astonishing truth about who it was Isaiah saw. From the context (John 12:37ff), we see that Isaiah saw *Jesus'* glory and spoke about *him* (v. 41)!

This holy Jesus, the Lord of hosts, is the Eternal One who reigns over everyone and everything. He had always *been* God. He had always been *with* God.

3. *Jesus was also the Creator of the universe.* As the second person of the Trinity, he spoke everything into existence by his powerful words. Paul wrote, "By him all things were created, in heaven and on earth, visible and invisible, whether thrones or dominions or rulers or authorities—all things were created through him and for him" (Colossians 1:16).

What Jesus Became

Read this description of "Jesus as God" in John 1:1–3, immediately dropping down to verse 14: "In the beginning was the Word, and the Word was with God, and the Word was God. He was in the beginning with God. All things were made through him, and without him was not any thing made that was made…" Then, "The Word became flesh and dwelt among us"!

Notice these stunning contrasts:

1. *Jesus became flesh.* The One who was the Eternal God "became flesh" (v. 14). The Holy Spirit could have led John to use a less bold word. He could have said, "The Word became a human being," but he didn't. The Holy Spirit picked a blunt word to get his point across: "The Word became flesh."

Sometimes, trying to be emphatic, we use the phrase, "real flesh and blood." That is the kind of blunt talk John is using. Jesus Christ was God-come-in-the-flesh.

Jesus' *incarnation* began with his conception and birth. The Eternal God had now taken on a human body, bound by time and space. The Ancient of Days now had a body that became tired, hungry, and thirsty. God-in-the-flesh felt pain and temptation. The Eternal One bled real blood and died a real death on the cross.

2. *Jesus became one of us.* The One who had lived in all eternity past "with God" willingly "dwelt among us." Isn't it jolting to realize that the Eternal God entered this world in a smelly stable?

In his classic book *Knowing God*, J. I. Packer observed, "The story is usually prettified when we tell it Christmas by Christmas, but it is really rather beastly and cruel."[6]

Packer was right, wasn't he? Jesus, the One who had enjoyed the perfect love of the Father, "Came to his own, and his own people did not receive him" (John 1:11).

Why was Jesus born in a stable? Because no one would give up his bed for a young woman in labor with the Son of Man. Jesus' birth foreshadowed the life he would live on this sin-infected planet. He would be rejected over and over by the very people to whom he had given life.

3. *Jesus became humbled.* The One who had lived for all eternity past as God (John 1:1), adopted a common life as the stepson of a Jewish carpenter. The One who had worn the royal robes of heaven took them off to be wrapped in baby clothes. The One who had sat on the throne of the universe had nowhere to lay his head. He who had enjoyed the praise of angelic beings calling "Holy, holy, holy," would endure the mob's angry cries, "Crucify him! Crucify him!"

4. Jesus became dependent. The One who had been the Creator of the Universe was now a dependent baby boy. The One who had spoken the universe into existence now made the soft cooing sounds of a newborn baby. The One who had sustained the universe by his divine power depended on a young Jewish woman to nurse him and change his diaper.

Henry Gariepy further illustrates the contrasts in his devotional book, *100 Portraits of Christ*:

> The Christ who walked the dusty roads of Galilee was the God who had roamed through the paths of galaxies. The Christ who lit the lakeside fire on which to cook breakfast for His tired, hungry disciples, had lit a billion stars and hung them across the midnight sky. He who asked the outcast for a drink had filled with water every river, lake, and ocean. Christ became God's self-disclosure. In Jesus, God entered humanity. Eternity invaded time.[7]

What kind of man is this? This Man, Jesus of Nazareth, is God-come-in-the-flesh. God came and lived in our world as a real human being. Jesus is God *incarnate.*

What Does Jesus' Incarnation Mean to You and Me?

In our quest to walk like Jesus, we may struggle to imagine how all this about Jesus' coming in the flesh applies to us. But following the incarnate Christ means this:

1. *Receiving salvation.* The ultimate impact of the incarnation of Jesus Christ is that we can have eternal salvation.

The apostle Paul reminded us in 1 Timothy 1:15, "The saying is trustworthy and deserving of full acceptance, that Christ Jesus came into the world to save sinners." Had Jesus not come into our world, there would be no salvation. And our acceptance or rejection of him determines our eternal destiny.

But there is another way the incarnation of Jesus impacts our lives as his followers.

2. *Living openly for Christ at all times.* The night before Jesus went to the cross to accomplish the salvation of his people, he prayed to

his Father, "As you sent me into the world, I have sent them into the world" (John 17:18). And, after Jesus rose to life following his death on the cross, he announced to his disciples, "As the Father has sent me, even so I am sending you" (John 20:21).

The calling of every follower of the incarnate Savior is to live incarnational lives—God's character on display in us among unbelievers and believers alike. We cannot hide in Christian ghettos, seeking minimal contact with the world. From the beginning, Jesus taught his followers, "You are the light of the world. A city set on a hill cannot be hidden. Nor do people light a lamp and put it under a basket, but on a stand, and it gives light to all in the house. In the same way, let your light shine before others, so that they may see your good works and give glory to your Father who is in heaven" (Matthew 5:14–16).

The apostle Peter was on the Galilean hillside that day, hearing the Savior explain the incarnational lifestyle he required of his followers. And Peter later wrote, "Keep your conduct among the Gentiles honorable, so that when they speak against you as evildoers, they may see your good deeds and glorify God on the day of visitation" (1 Peter 2:12).

Following the incarnate Lord Jesus means infiltrating our world in order to draw people's attention to God. Following him means reflecting the character of Christ in our schools, our workplaces, our neighborhoods, and our homes. Following him means not hiding from the world but shining for him. As our Savior's life did, our "incarnational lifestyle" will bring God glory.

Some of our incarnational outreach may focus on acts of mercy, of stepping into the various worlds of people in need and mirroring Christ's character. Jesus wants us to be his hands and feet in our hurting world. On judgment day he will say to those who have been faithful in this way, "Truly, I say to you, as you did it to one of the least of these my brothers, you did it to me" (Matthew 25:40).

We can mirror our Savior's character by befriending those who are struggling with discouragement, sickness, or the challenges of aging. Doing what we can to help them in their time of need brings glory to God.

We can mirror our Savior's character by coming alongside those who are wrestling with addictions. Doing what we can, firmly but lovingly, to help them find their hope in Christ brings glory to God.

We can mirror our Savior's character by entering the worlds of those who are socially ostracized at school or work. Doing what we can, by sitting with them and visiting with them in the cafeteria or break room, and by showing them the love of our Savior, brings glory to God.

We can mirror our Savior's character by moving out of our comfort zones and volunteering in such settings as a soup kitchen, a homeless shelter, a thrift store, a hospice ministry, or a nursing home.

Other incarnational opportunities may focus more directly on sharing the gospel. Many opportunities exist: befriending an immigrant who needs to hear the salvation story, serving Christ in a jail or prison, helping with Bible studies at a rescue mission, and so much more.

Doing what we can to encourage and give the hope of the gospel to those who need it most brings glory to God.

What kind of man is this, who willingly left the comforts of heaven and entered our sinful world? He is the One who also calls us to move out of our comfort zones to tell others about him.

May God help us see opportunities he has given us to mirror Jesus' willingness to leave his world for ours.

> Lord, please move me to rejoice with those who rejoice,
> to mourn with those who mourn.
> to live in harmony with people who may not be like me.
> Help me not to be proud
> but to be willing to associate with people of low position.
> Please change me that I might not be conceited
> but reflect my humble Savior.
>
> —Adapted from Romans 12:15–16

Discussion Questions

LIVING INCARNATIONALLY LIKE JESUS

1. Read aloud John 1:1–14 in two different versions or paraphrases of the Bible.

2. Explore what life would have been like for Jesus before he was conceived in Mary's womb. Read Isaiah 6:1–4. Write down and discuss your observations concerning the sights, sounds, and smells Jesus would have experienced in heaven.

3. What comes to your mind as you contrast Jesus' earthly life with his life before his incarnation?

4. Why did Jesus willingly come to this world "in the flesh?" Read Hebrews 2 as a catalyst for your thinking.

5. How might you live incarnationally by coming alongside hurting people? What opportunities for showing mercy are available to you?

6. What openings for sharing the gospel might you have—even if they would take you out of your comfort zone and into other people's worlds?

7. Add to your daily prayer journal this request: "Lord, show me today someone whose world I should enter to show the love of Christ and share the message of Christ."

Chapter 5

WALKING IN HOLINESS LIKE JESUS

EARLY IN JESUS' PUBLIC MINISTRY HE PURPOSEFULLY (SEE MATTHEW 3:13) walked out to the Jordan River and asked the prophet John to baptize him. John protested, arguing that he needed Jesus to baptize him, not the other way around. After all, John's baptism was an open sign of repentance.

But Jesus insisted. Essentially, he said, "We have to do this to follow God's plan."

Surely John still felt uneasy as he waded out into the Jordan with Jesus and baptized him. After all, John had been telling people about this One who was coming: "He who is coming after me is mightier than I, whose sandals I am not worthy to carry" (Matthew 3:11). But he did as Jesus commanded.

In that moment Jesus stood alongside all of fallen humanity. Though he himself was holy—without sin—he identified with us, showing himself to be the God-Man.

Then an amazing thing happened. Jesus was praying, and the enabling power of the Holy Spirit came down on him in visible form. His heavenly Father assured him of his approval: "You are my beloved Son," God said. "With you I am well pleased" (Luke 3:22). What a comforting and reassuring moment that must have been for Jesus!

However, immediately after that momentous event, the Holy Spirit led Jesus into the rocky, hot, arid Judean wilderness. What was he doing in a barren place like that?

What a far cry from the paradise the first Adam enjoyed in the garden of Eden! Jesus had a divine appointment. The Holy Spirit led him there for a specific purpose—to meet Satan head on. God sent his Son into the wilderness in order to test and prove his loyalty to his Father.

For forty days Jesus fasted. Alone with God, without even a bite of food to distract him, Jesus surely contemplated his mission on earth, communed with his loving heavenly Father, and prepared for the public ministry that lay ahead for the next three years.

Then Satan came.

Temptation Attack

Satan begins his attack when Jesus is hungry, weak, and tired. The enemy tempts Jesus, the second Adam or "last Adam" (1 Corinthians 15:45), in a way reminiscent of how he dealt with the first Adam. Satan does his best to sully the holiness of Jesus. Will Jesus abandon his dedication to his Father and pursue his own purposes and pleasures instead?

Three times Satan attacks, and three times Jesus resists.

1. *The temptation to be selfish.* For the enemy's first attack on Jesus he says, "If you are the Son of God, command this stone to become bread" (Luke 4:3). Can you imagine how hungry Jesus must have been after forty days of fasting? Each of the thousands of flat rocks within his gaze must have reminded him of the flat bread he had eaten nearly every day of his thirty years on this earth. Here Satan is attacking Jesus' loyalty to his heavenly Father by appealing to his physical appetite for food, just as he did with Adam and Eve (Genesis 3:6).

But Satan tries enticing Jesus to satisfy his legitimate desire for food in an illegitimate way. The enemy prefaces his appeal with the phrase, "If you are the Son of God." That could be translated, "Since you are the Son of God." Satan says, in effect, "Look, you're hungry. Take advantage of your Sonship! You don't have to wait for the Father to meet your needs. Maybe he won't! You have the power to satisfy yourself. Go ahead. You have the power. Use it. Satisfy yourself. Be selfish!"

How does Jesus respond to this temptation to satisfy himself illegitimately? He responds in holiness. The essence of holiness is to be dedicated to God and his purposes.

So it is significant that Jesus resists Satan by quoting from the book of the Bible that records Israel's wilderness temptations—and repeated failures—the book of Deuteronomy. Jesus' retort to the archenemy? "It is written: 'Man does not live by bread alone'" (8:3). Why would Jesus quote this particular verse? Jesus seems to be saying, "It is not really the material things that count in life. It is our trust in, and loyalty to, whatever God says."

Jesus implies that we are more than animals with physical appetites. We are spiritual beings in a special relationship with God himself. Our hope is not so much in the supply as in the Supplier, not so much in the gift as in the Giver. Jesus clearly resists Satan and maintains his holiness by giving the adversary this message: "I can trust my Father. My trust is in him more than what he provides. I don't need to take things into my own hands. I will not be selfish! I will be loyal to my heavenly Father."

2. *The temptation to be successful.* Jesus stands strong, but Satan is not done. He attacks again, seeking to lure Jesus away from his loyalty to his Father. In Luke 4:5–7 Satan shows Jesus a panorama of all the world's kingdoms, trying to shake Jesus' commitment to his Father's will and honor. Satan wants Jesus to abandon that pursuit and pursue his own glory.

Satan lies, saying that he himself owns all the kingdoms of the world. He tries to beguile Jesus with this proposition: "To you I will give all this authority and their glory, for it has been delivered to me, and I give it to whom I will" (Luke 4:6).

What an arrogant liar he is! According to Psalm 2, God promised all the nations to the Messiah, not to Satan. Nevertheless, the great deceiver tries to charm Jesus: "Just think. You can have all these kingdoms without enduring the shame and pain of the cross! Wouldn't that be great? You can have the crown without the cross. Here's a shortcut."

His enticing offer has one catch: its price: "If you, then, will worship me, it will all be yours" (Luke 4:7). Satan wants Jesus to worship him instead of honoring God the Father! But note how Jesus responds.

Once again Jesus refuses to compromise his holiness—his dedication to his heavenly Father. Instead of worshiping the devil, Jesus rebukes him by referring to Deuteronomy 6:13, "Worship the Lord your God and serve him only" (NIV). He was saying, "God alone is sovereign. He alone is worthy of our worship and service. No matter how costly, we must worship God alone."

Jesus did not come to this earth to be successful as the world defines success. He "came not to be served, but to serve, and to give his life as a ransom for many" (Matthew 20:28).

Jesus is not duped by Satan's "success scheme," circumventing the cross. Our Savior maintains his holiness—his loyalty to his heavenly Father. He is willing to follow the path the Father has laid out for him, no matter how humbling and painful.

3. *The temptation to be spectacular.* Through all this, Jesus remains loyal to his holy Father. He resists Satan's temptations to be selfish and to be successful. But the archenemy still is not ready to retreat from the wilderness battlefield.

Satan attacks Jesus again, this time tempting him to be spectacular. Leading Jesus to the highest point of the temple in Jerusalem, Satan says, "If you are the Son of God, throw yourself down from here, for it is written, 'He will command his angels concerning you, to guard you,' and 'On their hands they will bear you up, lest you strike your foot against a stone'" (Luke 4:9–11).

How audacious for Satan to use God's own words (Psalm 91:11–12) in his sinful schemes!

Can we hear echoes of the Serpent's hiss, tempting Adam and Eve? There, too, in tempting them to doubt God's care for them, the enemy misapplied God's words.

At the temple's pinnacle, isn't Satan again trying to plant doubt, saying in essence, "Jesus, are you sure your heavenly Father really cares about you? Can you truly trust his words of love and assurance? Maybe you ought to test his concern. Force the hand of God the Father! Make him prove his love for you. Do something spectacular just to make sure he really will protect you. Jump!"

Once more Jesus demonstrates his holiness—his unswerving allegiance to his heavenly Father. Once more he rejects the adversary's attack by quoting from Deuteronomy. Jesus recites Deuteronomy 6:16 in its appropriate context: "You shall not put the Lord your God to the test."

Although Adam failed to trust God's words to him, Jesus stood strong! We could paraphrase Jesus' response to Satan like this: "God's word is enough. I trust him. I don't need to put him to the test. That is not trust. That is presumption. Demanding that God do something in addition to his already revealed will in order to prove his love for me is not only unnecessary, it is offensive. Real trust never resorts to tricks. The Father's revealed will is enough for me. Get away from me, Satan! You won't pull me away from my heavenly Father. I will trust him. I will remain loyal."

Luke records an epilogue in verse 13, "When the devil had ended every temptation, he departed from him until an opportune time."

Through all these attacks, Jesus, the second Adam, stood as victor on the spiritual battlefield. Over and over, he demonstrated his holiness, his commitment to live for God's purposes and God's pleasure rather than his own.

Walking Like Jesus in Holiness

How does the story of Jesus' holiness impact you and me? How can we be like him, mirroring his holiness?

1. *We can reflect Jesus' holiness by claiming the great hope we have in Jesus.* He is our victorious leader! Even though the first Adam failed the test in the garden of Eden, Jesus, the last Adam, perfectly passed his test. His holiness—his dedication to his Father's priorities and pleasure—remained unmoved and untarnished. The first Adam failed. The last Adam conquered! Jesus is the One who "in every respect has been tempted as we are, yet without sin" (Hebrews 4:15).

As followers of Jesus, we too can know victory over sin and Satan. Paul tells us that no matter what the enemy throws at us, "in all these things we are more than conquerors through him who loved us" (Romans 8:37). As people who are "in Christ," we are no longer under the bondage of sin. Satan no longer has claims on us. In Christ, we can refuse to yield to Satan's evil schemes. God has "delivered us from the domain of darkness and transferred us to the kingdom of his beloved Son" (Colossians 1:13).

2. *We can reflect Jesus' holiness by remaining loyal to him.* Jesus' resolve there in the wilderness to remain loyal to his Father provides the su-

preme example of pursuing holiness. In John 5:30, Jesus explained, "I seek not my own will but the will of him who sent me." As believers, we are called *"to walk as Jesus did."* Just as our Lord did in the Judean wilderness, we too can resist the subtle schemes of Satan. God expects us to. We also have been called to be sons and daughters of God. The apostle Paul tells us to walk worthy of the calling we have received (Ephesians 4:1), living in obedient loyalty to our Father and Master.

3. *We can reflect Jesus' holiness by using the Word of God to resist temptation.* Satan will tempt us to be selfish, successful, and spectacular, even as he did Adam and Jesus. But our Savior showed us how to emerge victorious.

Scripture is the sword in our hands for battling our archenemy. When we know and use God's Word to answer Satan's schemes, we too can gain the victory.

Personally, over the years, God's Word has empowered me to fight Satan's schemes to turn my heart away from God and toward sinful lusts. How kind the Holy Spirit has been to remind me of the Scripture, "You are not your own, for you were bought with a price. So glorify God in your body" (1 Corinthians 6:19–20). What hope-giving power God's Word has in our lives, providing his strength when we feel our weakness.

Knowing and using God's Word helps us maintain an unswerving loyalty to his priorities, purpose, and pleasure. Like Jesus, we can find that doing the will of our Father and accomplishing his work will increasingly be our delight (John 4:34).

Satan is both subtle and bold. Yet, as children of God, walking in the Spirit with the sword of God's Word in our hands, "we are more than conquerors through him who loved us" (Romans 8:37).

And though this world, with devils filled,
Should threaten to undo us,
We will not fear, for God hath willed
His truth to triumph through us:
The Prince of Darkness grim—
We tremble not for him;

His rage we can endure,
For lo, his doom is sure,
One little word shall fell him.

—Martin Luther

Discussion Questions

WALKING IN HOLINESS LIKE JESUS

1. In your own words, what is the essence of holiness?

2. What are some ways Satan tempts believers to abandon their loyalty to God in order to be selfish, successful, and spectacular?

3. When might Christians be most vulnerable to Satan's attacks?

4. How can Jesus' victory over Satan impact the way you respond to temptations?

5. With what truths should we arm ourselves as followers of Jesus in order to withstand the seductions of Satan? To prompt your thinking, read these passages: Romans 6:11–14; Ephesians 6:10–18; James 4:7; 1 Peter 5:8–9.

6. What hope is there when we have yielded to Satan's temptations? See Proverbs 28:13 and 1 John 1:9. In your quiet time with God, read Psalm 32 and Psalm 51. Talk to God about your desire to be forgiven and to live a life of holiness.

7. How can we help one another in the body of Christ to resist Satan's subtle schemes? See Ephesians 6:18 and Hebrews 3:12–14.

Chapter 6
ACCEPTING OTHERS LIKE JESUS

In the early days of our church, we were excited when an unexpected visitor attended our worship service. My wife and I invited this shabbily dressed, older widower to lunch at our home. The conversation was pleasant, but at the end of our time together our guest told us, with lowered voice and lowered eyes, that he would probably not be back to our church. When I asked why, he answered, "I don't think I would fit in. Everyone else is better dressed than me, and they all sound so smart. I never even finished high school."

His decision made me sad, but I couldn't disagree with him. Our church had been founded by a small group of current and former students from the nearby Christian college and theological seminary. Most of our church members were young, well-dressed, and well-educated. In those first few years of our church's existence, we were a rather uniform church. We were so much alike that we didn't even consider how a visitor who was different might feel. For the first time as a young pastor, I began to pray passionately for God to change our church—to bring a diversity that reflected his diverse kingdom.

Sadly, in spite of our apologies and encouragements, our guest did not return. But by God's grace that encounter did effect change. A growing number of our church members began making a conscious effort to befriend people who were different from them. Over time, our church, though still not as diverse as we would like it to be, began to more clearly reflect our community.

How diverse is your local church? In Western culture, our churches may consist of people from various backgrounds:

We differ in race, ethnicity, first language, education level, vocation, marital status, age, and socioeconomic situation.

We differ in salvation histories. Some were saved as children. Some came to know Christ as teens or college students. Still others committed themselves to Jesus when they were older. Some grew up in Christian homes. Others found redemption after long years of deep immorality.

We differ in convictions and preferences regarding political parties, social issues, styles of music, styles of clothing, and Bible translations!

Yet we all profess to believe in and follow the same Lord. We all claim to be part of one body of believers.

How can such a diverse group ever live and function with peace and unity? How can we work together to promote the cause of Christ in our own community and generation, let alone take the gospel to the nations?

Is it any wonder that some churches experience tension and even painful church splits? We are not the first generation of Christians to struggle with maintaining unity in the midst of diversity.

Diversity among the Apostles

Jesus personally chose a diverse group to be his apostles. His twelve closest disciples were far from a homogenous fraternity.

Jesus' disciples represented a variety of personality types. For example, Peter strikes us as a true extrovert, always ready to speak his mind, always ready to act. His brother Andrew, however, seemed to be an introvert, quiet and reserved.

Jesus also selected men from opposite ends of the political spectrum. He chose Simon the Zealot to join his band of followers. The designation *Zealot* meant Simon was a fanatical Jewish patriot, passionately opposing the Roman occupiers.

Matthew, on the other hand, had been a tax collector before he met Jesus. He had actually collaborated with the Roman government in his despised but lucrative occupation. Imagine the discussions Simon and Matthew had as they sat around the campfire in the evenings.

How did Jesus' diverse band of apostles ever get along with one another? They were not a haphazard collection of volunteers. Jesus chose them, knowing full well their differences.

The night before he died on the cross, Jesus reminded this diverse group, "You did not choose me, but I chose you" (John 15:16). He accepted extroverts as well as introverts. He accepted political conservatives as well as political liberals. The unifying factor was not similar personality types, political persuasions, or other characteristics. The unifying factor was Jesus himself.

Diversity in a New Testament Church

In the apostle Paul's day, the local church in Rome—a church made up of believers with widely varied backgrounds and convictions—struggled with unity and mutual acceptance. What made that quest so challenging? In Romans 14 and 15, Paul described two noticeably different camps with opposite convictions regarding diet and days.

- *Camp 1: The conservatives.* These believers had strong convictions regarding not eating certain foods and not doing certain things on designated days. Paul referred to them as people with weak faith. Most likely people with Jewish backgrounds, these believers had trouble trusting the sufficiency of Christ's fulfillment of the Old Testament laws. They thought it necessary to bolster the work of Christ with their own law keeping. They had difficulty letting go of lifelong practices, such as dietary restrictions as well as observances of the Sabbath and other holy days.

- *Camp 2: The liberals.* These believers had strong convictions regarding their freedom to eat any kind of food and to do a variety of things on any given day of the week. They had a strong confidence in the sufficiency of Christ's fulfillment of the Law. Most likely, this group was made up primarily of people with Gentile backgrounds. However, some Christians with Jewish backgrounds were also in this group. Paul was an ethnic Jew (even being trained as a Pharisee), but counted himself in this latter group (Romans 15:1). He said emphatically, "I know and am persuaded in the Lord Jesus that nothing is unclean in itself" (Romans 14:14). Paul referred to this second group as the "stronger brothers."

- *Commonalities.* What did these two very different groups have in common?

1. Both groups were made up of genuine believers who sincerely desired to please God (Romans 14:3, 13). Paul said both groups followed their convictions, doing so as to the Lord (v. 6).

2. Each group, however, criticized those on the other side. They looked at the others with contempt (v. 10), distancing themselves except to debate.

The weaker Christians looked down their noses at the stronger Christians. We might even imagine the weaker believers muttering, "Crazy bunch of liberals!" And they kept their distance.

Equally guilty, the stronger Christians criticized their weaker brothers and sisters. We might imagine the more liberal believers grumbling about the "crazy legalists" and their stringent scruples concerning diet and days.

3. Another commonality Paul mentioned repeatedly is that all believers—no matter which camp they were in—would give an account to God himself for their lives (vv. 4 and 10–12).

Apparently, people on both sides were erecting relational walls over these issues. Maybe they asked, "Why should I be friends with those people? I know I'm right, and they're wrong!"

Paul's Counsel to Diverse Churches

So how did Paul counsel this divided church?

First, he told them not to look down on brothers and sisters whose convictions differ from theirs—because God had accepted both groups. In essence Paul said, "Stop it!" Then he pointedly asked, "Who are you to pass judgment on the servant of another?" (Romans 14:3–4).

Second, Paul made it clear that not everyone would agree on these "disputable matters" (v. 1 NIV). He never said the two groups must ultimately agree with each other. He never asked one group to abandon its convictions (even though he makes no secret of his own view on the matters of diet and days). And he never called for a compromise position. (See Romans 14 and 15.)

But the apostle did call for the church to stop their criticism and judgment.

The responsibility to judge belongs to God himself. So Paul's counsel to us, as well, is not to usurp God's role regarding disputable matters. "You, then, why do you judge your brother? Or why do you look down on your brother? For we will all stand before God's judgment seat" (14:10). While God calls us to stand solidly on the clear teachings of the Bible, he also commands us to not add our own rules to God's Word. (See Proverbs 30:5–6.) We dare not erect barriers that Jesus, the head of the Church, never erected.

In our churches today, we may not quibble with fellow believers over what food to eat or what special days to observe, but we can usually find plenty of other things to dispute.

Some years ago, a man in our church, a former member of the military, was strenuously advocating that we hang an American flag at the front of our auditorium. I recall the anxiety in my soul as I asked to meet with him. He was obviously passionately patriotic, and he was also a fairly recent convert, so I wanted to be clear but gentle in my conversation.

I thanked him for his service to our country but then asked him to consider those who attend our church who are not citizens of our country—international businesspeople in our community on temporary assignment, college students from other countries, as well as high-school exchange students. I asked him, "Do you think God really wants us to be a 'national' church? Would that resonate with his agenda for reaching the world with the gospel?"

God showed mercy, and this newer believer agreed and embraced God's agenda of reaching diverse people with the gospel. Rather than wasting time and energy judging Christians who are not like us, how much better to invest our time and energy pursuing peace and Christian growth in the church. Paul challenges each of us to "make every effort to do what leads to peace and mutual edification" (v. 19 NIV).

Rather than wasting our time and energy promoting our own convictions or showing people on the other side how wrong they are, how much better to ask these questions: "Will my attitude, comment, or action promote the unity of our local body? Will this promote the spiritual growth of my brothers and sisters in Christ?"

For those of us who want to walk like Jesus, our goal is not to please ourselves but to patiently accept fellow believers with differing views in a way that will build them up spiritually. This is especially true if we consider ourselves one of the "stronger" ones (Romans 15:1–2).

Paul offers a blessing upon the church that can help us live in peace and harmony: "May the God of endurance and encouragement grant you to live in such harmony with one another, in accord with Christ Jesus, that together you may with one voice glorify the God and Father of our Lord Jesus Christ" (Romans 15:5–6).

Notice these keys for harmonious relationships in the church: endurance and encouragement, which comes from God.

Our commitment to following Jesus in challenging situations entails this command: "Welcome one another as Christ has welcomed you, for the glory of God" (15:7).

The word *welcome* means to take another to yourself in an embrace or to take someone into friendship. The concept is not mere tolerance but genuinely embracing the other as a friend and as a brother or sister in Christ.

Jesus, Our Motivation for Accepting One Another

Jesus is our *motivation* for accepting Christians who differ with us on various matters. When we thoughtfully reflect on the work of Christ, we realize that he has accepted all kinds of people into his kingdom: Jew and Gentile, slave and free, male and female, rich and poor, young and old, people from morally upright backgrounds and people from decadent lifestyles. They all came into the kingdom by means of the same Savior shedding the same blood and extending the same grace. Not one of us was more acceptable than another when Christ saved us.

How dare we communicate through our words and demeanor, "Well, maybe Jesus accepted that person, but I'm sure not going to!" What audacity to reject someone Jesus accepted at the cost of his own precious blood!

So, when we're tempted to put down our differing brothers and sisters, how much better to reflect on the cross: Look what it cost my precious Savior to accept them! Look what it cost him to accept *me*!

Regarding the Roman Christians' disputes, Paul said that insensitivity and lack of acceptance can destroy our fellow believers "for whom Christ died" (Romans 14:15). The same is true in our disputes today.

And in verse 20, he also says insensitivity and lack of acceptance can destroy God's work: "Do not destroy the work of God for the sake of [_____]." We can fill in the blank with our situation.

Jesus, Our Model for Accepting One Another

But how does all this work, practically speaking? Jesus is not only our *motivation* for accepting those with differing convictions; he is also our *model*. Paul wrote, "Welcome one another as Christ has welcomed you" (Romans 15:7).

1. *Jesus never sought to please himself.* Instead, out of love for others, he willingly endured the insults other people deserved (v. 3). Walking like Jesus means to "die to self"—die to our own preferences. Then, out of a loving concern for our brothers and sisters who are different from us, we can reach out humbly with open arms and welcome them.

2. *Jesus welcomed people whom society considered unacceptable.* Into his circle of followers, he called the physically disabled, Gentiles, women and children, prostitutes, and even tax collectors. And he has accepted the likes of you and me!

3. *Jesus left no one out.* Christ's kingdom has such breadth! He died for people of every race, ethnic background, socioeconomic status, and age. He left no one out.

When we truly recognize how precious each of our fellow believers is to him, we can accept them all, regardless of their backgrounds, preferences, and convictions. True Christians "walk as Jesus did" (1 John 2:6), accepting believers who do not share all their convictions on peripheral matters. Accepting others might not be comfortable and might not be popular. It certainly wasn't for Jesus. But he did it because it reflected his Father's character. It brought glory to God. Dare we do any less?

The Benefit of Accepting One Another

The ultimate result and benefit of accepting one another is that it honors God and brings him glory. Paul tells us that welcoming people unlike ourselves brings glory to God (Romans 15:7). Our Lord deliberately chose to put his glory on display by saving people from all kinds of backgrounds and forming them into "one new people" (Ephesians 2:15 NLT).

Jesus Christ came to pour out his grace on both Jews and Gentiles. This was always part of his plan. He created one new people out of two. Together, we are one body: Christ reconciled to God both ethnic groups by means of his death on the cross. There, he put to death our hostility toward each other (Ephesians 2:15–16). Can't he do the same with us in our differences?

Through the uniting of his people, the church, God demonstrated his wisdom and eternal purpose to all the heavenly beings. (See Ephesians 3:10–11.)

Think about this: God deliberately saves people of diverse backgrounds so that he can put his own glorious power and wisdom on display. He wants everyone to be impressed by how he can form one new people out of diverse believers. Accomplishing this in the church brings him praise and glory.

So, when we withhold fellowship from those whom Christ has chosen to include, we are undermining his goal of displaying his glory to everyone. But when we accept our brothers and sisters, becoming one heart and voice, we bring praise to God (Romans 15:6–7).

Jesus chose to accept undeserving sinners of differing stripes so that he could bring praise to his Father. God is making something entirely new. He wants everyone to be impressed with his wisdom and ability to bring diverse people together. Why then would we choose to run counter to his purposes by shunning those who differ from us in their convictions on disputable matters?

What a joy it must be for God when he sees a church filled with people who don't necessarily see every issue the same but nevertheless accept one another, just as Christ has accepted them!

Now to him who is able to do far more abundantly
than all that we ask or think,
according to the power at work within us,
to him be glory in the church and in Christ Jesus
throughout all generations, forever and ever. Amen.

—Ephesians 3:20–21

Discussion Questions

ACCEPTING OTHERS LIKE JESUS

1. Read Romans 14:1 through 15:7. What were some of the differences that challenged the church in Rome?

2. Name some of the diverse convictions you have noticed in your own church.

3. Give some examples of disputable matters in our culture, other than those at the beginning of the chapter.

4. In what ways does focusing on Christ's acceptance of us impact our readiness to accept Christians who differ from us?

5. How is the unity (or disunity) in your own church impacting the corporate testimony your church has in your community? Read John 17:20–23; Ephesians 2:15–16; Ephesians 3:10–11 before discussing the answer to this question.

6. How can you help improve the unity of your church? (For example, is there someone "different" in the church whom you could befriend? In what ways can you take the initiative in reaching across the barriers that keep people apart?)

7. Write out a prayer for your church, using the thoughts of Romans 15:5–7.

Chapter 7

SHOWING COMPASSION LIKE JESUS

ONE MORNING I STOPPED BY THE SPARSE AND FILTHY APARTMENT OF an alcoholic man with whom several of us in the church had been sharing the gospel. I spotted a half-empty bottle of malt liquor on his dirty table and asked, "Sam,[8] is that what you've had for breakfast?" When he nodded sheepishly, I said, "Come on. Let's get you a real breakfast."

During the short trip to the restaurant, I lost my own appetite. I had to pull off to the side of the road as Sam lost the malt liquor rebelling in his otherwise empty stomach.

Soon Sam and I stood, waiting to be seated, in full view of a room full of fellow diners. The few minutes we waited crawled by as I wondered what the people around us were thinking. Sam was disheveled, unshaven, dirty—and yes, smelly. Standing beside him, I became concerned about my own reputation. We live in a small town. People recognize one another. I'm a pastor, and I have a reputation to uphold. What would people think of me standing with such a loser?

Jesus' Compassionate Identity

Our loving Savior never thought like that. And his compassion puzzled John the Baptist. Stories about Jesus' preaching and miracles were finding their way to John in prison. There, in Herod's fortress prison of Machaerus, east of the Dead Sea, the prophet wondered what these seemingly incongruous reports meant.

John had passionately proclaimed a Messiah of wrath and judgment to the crowds who had ventured into the Judean desert: "He who is mightier than I is coming, the strap of whose sandals I am not worthy to untie," John said. "He will baptize you with the Holy Spirit and fire. His winnowing fork is in his hand, to clear his threshing floor and to gather the wheat into his barn, but the chaff he will burn with unquenchable fire" (Luke 3:16–17).

Incredibly, though, this Jesus of Nazareth was not clearing the spiritual threshing floor nor burning up chaff with unquenchable fire. He was healing sick people and preaching a gospel of salvation. Bible commentator Frederick Bruner wrote about this stage of Jesus' ministry:

> Jesus has not yet attacked any of the reigning political or economic powers; in his miracles he has simply picked up the pieces left by evil forces. Today, Jesus' work would be derisively called "an ambulance ministry," picking up the crushed victims of evil structures but failing to combat head-on those evil structures themselves.... Jesus is out in the sticks healing sick, "insignificant" little individuals here and there, but not doing much to change the basic structural problems in Israel's life.... The whole religio-ideological system seems thoroughly unthreatened by Jesus' do-goodism in the hills. What is more, John (the propagandist of the New Order) is in prison, and Herod (the embodiment of the oppressive Establishment) is still on the throne and is in fact about to have John's head. What kind of Messiah is this...?[9]

John wondered if he had been wrong about the coming Messiah. Maybe Jesus wasn't the One. John wanted clarification. So he sent two of his own pupils on the long journey north to Galilee to ask Jesus this one crucial question, "Are you the one who is to come, or shall we look for another?" (Matthew 11:3).

Jesus' reply may have surprised John, but it was clear. It characterized Jesus as the *compassionate* Messiah. Alluding to God's prophecies (Isaiah 35:5–6 and 61:1), Jesus answered, "Go and tell John what you hear and see: the blind receive their sight and the lame walk, lepers are cleansed and the deaf hear, and the dead are raised up, and the poor have good news preached to them. And blessed is the one who is not offended by me" (Matthew 11:4–6). John the Baptist had not been wrong in his descriptions of the coming Messiah, but he was unaware that the ministries of wrath and judgment would be carried out primarily at the Messiah's *second* coming. Jesus assured John that he, Jesus, was indeed the Messiah, and his credentials focused primarily on compassion (especially during this, his first coming). Marks of compassion were what identified him as the Messiah. What Isaiah had prophesied hundreds of years before[10] was now being fulfilled in Jesus of Nazareth. As we read the Gospel accounts of his earthly ministry, we're undoubtedly gripped by story after story of Jesus' compassion. Scottish pastor William Blaikie wrote in 1876, "No feature of our Lord's earthly career is more conspicuous, or more likely to arrest every reader of his life, than the tenderness of his feeling for the woes and suffering of men."[11]

How Did Jesus Illustrate Compassion?

Jesus truly cared for people, and he showed it. Time after time we read that Jesus was "moved with compassion" when he saw hurting people, and he poured out his tender mercy on them. Here are a few examples out of many:

1. *Jesus showed compassion for those with physical hurts.* The Gospels tell the story of two blind beggars who cried out to Jesus, "Lord, have mercy on us, Son of David!" (Matthew 20:31). Even though the crowd tried to hush the beggars, Jesus heard their plea and asked what they wanted him to do. They replied, "Lord, let our eyes be opened."

Matthew says, "Jesus in pity touched their eyes, and immediately they recovered their sight and followed him" (Matthew 20:32–34).

2. *Jesus showed compassion for those with emotional hurts.* Heading into the town of Nain, a happy procession of Jesus and his followers met a sad funeral procession heading out toward the town cemetery. A widow, overwhelmed with grief upon grief, followed the coffin. She had already buried her husband, and now she was burying her son—her only son.

Luke reports that Jesus "had compassion on her." Then imagine the tenderness in his eyes when he said, "Do not weep" (Luke 7:12–

13). What a comfort it is, when our hearts are broken with grief, to remember that our Savior sees, our Savior cares!

3. *Jesus showed compassion for the marginalized and ostracized.* His compassion reached out to people society rejected. Tax collectors were some of the most unwelcome people in Jewish society, yet Jesus went against the grain and reached out to these despised individuals.

In Matthew's Gospel, he recalled that exciting evening when he had a dinner at his own home for his old friends and his new Master. The religious establishment could not believe that Jesus would associate with these pariahs of Jewish society. The judgmental Pharisees asked Jesus' disciples, "Why does your teacher eat with tax collectors and sinners?" Jesus responded from a heart of compassionate mercy: "Those who are well have no need of a physician, but those who are sick. Go and learn what this means: 'I desire mercy, and not sacrifice.' For I came not to call the righteous, but sinners" (Matthew 9:11–13).

Others who lived with the pain of rejection also personally received Jesus' unexpected compassion. Among them were prostitutes (Luke 9:36–50), children (Mark 10:13–16), and the outcast lepers (Mark 1:40–45).

Mark relates a beautiful picture of our Lord in Mark 1:40–41. A man who had leprosy fell on his knees before Jesus and begged Jesus to heal him—if he was willing.

Jesus, *filled with compassion*, reached out and touched the leper. "I am willing," Jesus said. "Be clean!"

What tenderness Jesus felt for these people who were forced to live on the fringes of society, cut off from normal loving relationships. Jesus was filled with compassion for this leper, whom everyone else avoided. Jesus loved him. Jesus touched him. Jesus healed him.

4. *Jesus showed compassion for the spiritually lost.* This is where we see Jesus' compassion most deeply. At times, Jesus would look upon a crowd of people on their way to God's eternal judgment, and his heart would break. (See Matthew 23:37.) Matthew recalled one time Jesus saw the crowds and had compassion on them "because they were harassed and helpless, like sheep without a shepherd." So Jesus taught his disciples to pray to the Lord of the harvest to raise up workers who would reach these lost sheep (Matthew 9:35–38).

Jesus cared deeply about lost people. Have you noted how Jesus dealt with the rich young ruler? "Jesus, looking at him, loved him" (Mark 10:21). Truly, Jesus had compassion on people who were spiritually lost—whether a respected religious young man or a woman who had earned her bad reputation with her sinful lifestyle (John 4:7–42).

Considering all this, John the Baptist had good reason to be reassured. Jesus was indeed the Messiah. His life and ministry of compassion marked him as God's Anointed One. Jesus' heart went out to people suffering physically, people grieving the loss of loved ones, people rejected by their families and neighbors, and people who were spiritually lost.

But the Savior's compassion cost him greatly.

1. *It cost him his physical and emotional energy.* Exhaustion marked his days as he healed hurting people and told them the good news of his grace.

2. *It cost him his reputation.* He was slandered with the mean-spirited epithet, "friend of sinners."

3. *It cost him his life.* Jesus' ultimate act of compassion was his death on that Roman cross. He willingly gave up his own life for totally undeserving sinners. Yes, tell the world this: Jesus is the compassionate Savior.

How Can We Demonstrate His Compassion?

We live in a world marked by pain and suffering. Yet we have been rescued by the saving compassion of Jesus our Savior. So God calls us to reflect his heart in all our thoughts and actions—to walk as Jesus did. He gives us many opportunities every day to mirror the heart of our Master, and he wants us to be increasingly moved with compassion.

The apostle Paul wrote to the Philippians, "God knows how much I love you and long for you with the tender compassion of Christ Jesus." (1:8 NLT). When we cultivate a heart like that, the compassion of Christ can flow through us whenever we see hurting people, grieving people, rejected people, and lost people.

God calls us, like our compassionate Savior, to willingly sacrifice our energy, our resources, our reputations, and even our lives for the benefit of those who most need our love.

On that day when I stood uncomfortably close to Sam in public view, waiting to be seated at the restaurant, the Holy Spirit rebuked me for my pride and lack of compassion. A flood of shame flowed over me. The Spirit reminded me of this truth: Jesus was not ashamed to call you his brother! He showed compassion on you by coming to this earth to save you, sacrificing everything—his reputation, even his life. (See Hebrew 2:11.)

I thought, *Larry, are you not willing to sacrifice your reputation to show Christ's compassion to this alcoholic?*

When the waitress finally seated my friend and me, I silently prayed for the Lord's forgiveness. How kind—how compassionate—of him to forgive me of my pride.

The words of Andrew Murray, written many years ago, still ring true: "We who owe everything to his compassion, who profess ourselves his followers, who walk in his footsteps and bear his image, oh, let us exhibit his compassion to the world. We can do it. He lives in us; His Spirit works in us. Let us with much prayer and firm faith look to his example as the sure promise of what we can be."[12]

One day Jesus' followers will ask, "Lord, when did we see you hungry and feed you, or thirsty and give you drink? And when did we see you a stranger and welcome you, or naked and clothe you? And when did we see you sick or in prison and visit you?"

Then the King will answer them, "Truly, I say to you, as you did it to one of the least of these my brothers, you did it to me" (from Matthew 25:31–40).

> O, to be like Thee! full of compassion,
> Loving, forgiving, tender and kind;
> Helping the helpless, cheering the fainting,
> Seeking the wandering sinner to find.
> O, to be like Thee! O, to be like Thee,
> Blessed Redeemer, pure as Thou art!

Come in Thy sweetness, come in Thy fullness;
Stamp Thine own image deep on my heart.

—Thomas O. Chisholm

Discussion Questions

SHOWING COMPASSION LIKE JESUS

1. What is one of your favorite stories in the Bible that describes Jesus showing compassion? Why does that story grip you?

2. What did Jesus' compassion cost him?

3. Relate the story of someone showing compassion to you during a difficult time in your life.

4. Make a list of ideas for ministries of compassionate mercy that your church might become involved in and ways to implement them.

5. List some ideas for gospel (evangelistic) compassion ministries that your church might become involved in and ways to implement them.

6. Who (or what kind of people) is God placing on your heart—people to whom you can show the compassion of Jesus?

7. Read aloud Matthew 25:31–40. Let that passage prime your heart as you ask God to transform you into a Christ-reflecting person, walking with compassion as Jesus did.

Chapter 8
SUFFERING LIKE JESUS

"Now is your chance, David! Kill him!"

David the warrior and his soldiers are hiding from King Saul in the back of a cave. Time and again, David had endured suffering—undeserved suffering—from the hand of King Saul. How many times had the jealous king sought to kill the man God had chosen to replace him? Now David is on the run again, trying to stay a step ahead of his murderous pursuer. This had been another narrow escape as David and his men sheltered in the cave. How tempting it would be for David to carry out the whispered urging of his men! Finally, he could get vengeance on the man who had made his life miserable.

Saul had gone into the very cave David was hiding in not because he suspected David to be there, but merely because "nature called." (See 1 Samuel 24.)

Stealthily, sword in hand, David creeps closer and closer to his unsuspecting tormentor. Now is David's opportunity to make Saul pay. Could David do it? Would he?

Jesus' Familiarity with Suffering

Another horribly mistreated figure comes to mind. Seven hundred years before Jesus Christ was born in a stable, Isaiah spoke these prophetic words about the yet-to-come Messiah: "He was despised and rejected by men, a man of sorrows and acquainted with grief" (Isaiah 53:3). Did this prophecy prove to be true? Oh, yes. During Jesus' thirty-three years in this sin-saturated world, he became very familiar with suffering.

1. *Jesus suffered physically.* During his time on earth, Jesus experienced *physical* suffering of various kinds. During his forty days of temptation in the wilderness, he suffered great hunger and thirst. After he called his disciples, he knew the bone-aching exhaustion that came from long, hard days of ministering to people. In the last hours of his life, he drank fully from the cup of suffering found in the diabolical execution known as crucifixion.

2. *Jesus suffered emotionally.* Jesus also endured the soul-deep ache of rejection. The apostle John, one of Jesus' closest companions, noted this painful reality: "He came to his own, and his own people did not receive him" (John 1:11). After a brief period of popularity, the time came when many of his disciples quit following him (John 6:66). This painful rejection culminated on that afternoon when midnight fell. As Jesus looked down from the cross, he saw that, of all his many previous followers, only John and a handful of women remained.

Then, the ultimate anguish of rejection came as Jesus cried out, "My God, my God, why have you forsaken me?" (Matthew 27:46).

3. *Jesus suffered spiritually.* His was a type of spiritual suffering unknown to you and me. He was sinless, yet he had to live day in and day out in a world polluted by sin. He had lived in a sinless, curse-free heaven before coming to this earth. How he must have suffered deep in his soul to see and feel the effects of sin and its curse all around him every day.

And ultimately, he suffered in a way incomprehensible and inexplicable to us. Jesus, the One who knew no sin, actually became sin for us (2 Corinthians 5:21). What anguish did the Sinless One feel as his pure soul and body carried the dreadful weight of sin from all the people he created? Contrary to the expectations of most of his contemporaries, regarding the Messiah, Jesus was marked by suffering—physically, emotionally, and spiritually.

How Jesus Might Have Responded to Suffering

Did Jesus have some kind of spiritual anesthetic that kept him from feeling the pain of suffering? No. In fact, being sinless, his senses and his emotions would have been perfect. Jesus would have felt every type of suffering perfectly. No sin dulled his feelings. No calluses encased his heart. And no spiritual anesthetic took away the pain.

Here are some common ways people respond to suffering. Did Jesus?

1. *Retaliation.* Did our Savior use his divine prerogative and *strike back* at those who hurt him? No. Think about it. Jesus suffered in multiple ways, yet he never took revenge against those who hurt him. Jesus never fought fire with fire. He never responded to suffering—even undeserved suffering—with sinful retaliation. Not even once.

Jesus perfectly fulfilled Isaiah's characterization of the anticipated Messiah—that he did "no violence" (Isaiah 53:9).

2. *Abusive comebacks.* Think about the horrendous insults hurled at the Sinless One during his earthly mission: blasphemer, glutton, drunkard, demon-possessed, deceiver of the people, friend of sinners, and more.

Imagine Peter, standing in the high priest's courtyard on that dreadful night Peter betrayed Jesus. Maybe the apostle overheard the insults coming from the religious leaders. The Gospel writer Mark describes the scene: "The chief priests accused him of many things. And Pilate again asked him, 'Have you no answer to make? See how many charges they bring against you.' But Jesus made no further answer, so that Pilate was amazed" (Mark 15:3–5).

As our Savior hung on the cross, these same vicious people continued their assaults, this time joined by the crowds who came to gawk and spew their hatred upon Jesus. In Mark's Gospel, he wrote,

Those who passed by derided him, wagging their heads and saying, "Aha! You who would destroy the temple and re-build it in three days, save yourself, and come down from the cross!" So also the chief priests with the scribes mocked him to one another, saying, "He saved others; he cannot save himself. Let the Christ, the King of Israel, come down now from the cross that we may see and believe." Those who were crucified with him also reviled him. (Mark 15:29–32).

Yet our Lord didn't respond. Jesus fulfilled Isaiah's prophecy about the Messiah, that although he suffered greatly, he didn't open his mouth (Isaiah 53:7). Isaiah also said there would be "no deceit in his mouth" (v. 9). Nothing untrue.

Even when he was suffering severely, Jesus never sought to protect himself or alleviate his pain by resorting to lies, deceit, or any kind of abusive comebacks. Peter wrote, "When he was reviled [subjected to verbal abuse], he did not revile in return; when he suffered, he did not threaten" (1 Peter 2:23, brackets added), or as the NIV puts it, "he made no threats."

How could Jesus absorb all that horrible suffering without retaliating? He certainly felt the pain. He was not anesthetized physically, emotionally, or spiritually. How could he bear up "under the pain of unjust suffering?"

How Jesus Did Respond to Suffering

The key to understanding this aspect of our Lord's life is found in this one short phrase, that Jesus "continued entrusting himself to him who judges justly" (1 Peter 2:23). What does that mean?

First, we need a little background. When Peter wrote that Jesus "committed no sin," he was echoing Isaiah 53:9's description of Messiah: He did no violence, and he made no threats.

Matthew's Gospel describes that horrible crucifixion morning: Jesus was flogged, stripped, mocked, spit upon, and beaten on his thorn-crowned head (27:26–31). He deserved none of this suffering. He had done nothing to hurt those people who were hurting him. Though he was severely suffering—and that, unjustly, he didn't make threats.

Jesus never went against his heavenly Father. He never sinned. This is a clear teaching of the New Testament writers about our Lord.[13]

- Pilate could find no sin in Jesus.

- One of the thieves on the cross declared Jesus to be innocent of all wrong.

- Peter, who spent much time with Jesus and saw him in a variety of situations, could also vouch for the fact that Jesus never sinned.

No one can argue with this observation from James: "We all stumble in many ways. And if anyone does not stumble in what he says, he is a perfect man" (3:2). Surely, Jesus was a perfect man.

In contrast to the ways we often handle suffering, how did Jesus respond?

1. *Jesus responded with forgiveness.* Instead of retaliatory threats, the words flowing from the lips of our suffering Savior, were "Father, forgive them" (Luke 23:34). How could he *forgive*? How could Jesus absorb all that horrible suffering? His deity had not numbed him to physical, emotional, or spiritual pain. So how could he bear up under the pain of unjust suffering? Read on.

2. *Jesus responded with faith.* We usually think of putting our faith *in* Jesus. We don't think of Jesus himself having faith. Yet here is an explicit expression of Jesus responding to his many types of pain by "entrusting himself" to his heavenly Father. This was no grim resignation on Jesus' part. This was his willful choice. He chose to take his painful situations and entrust them—entrust *himself*—to his trustworthy Father. That's what faith is. That's what faith does.

Rather than seeking to alleviate the pain he was feeling, he took his pain to the One who truly cared. Rather than seeking to take justice into his own hands, he put his faith in the One who judges justly. Even though Jesus had the power and the right to retaliate, he chose not to.

Jesus had faith in his Father, sure that his Father would do the right thing at the right time. That's the basis for what the apostle Paul wrote to the Romans: "Repay no one evil for evil… Beloved, never avenge yourselves, but leave it to the wrath of God, for it is written, 'Vengeance is mine, I will repay, says the Lord'" (12:17, 19).

How Can We Respond to Suffering the Way Jesus Did?

Retaliation and abusive comebacks are natural human responses. And, like our Savior, we believers are certainly acquainted with grief and suffering (though to a lesser degree). We live in a world infected by sin and dominated by the curse. We suffer physically, relationally, and spiritually. But, in practical terms, if we're seeking to walk like Jesus did, how shall we respond?

- Should we live by the bumper-sticker philosophy, "I don't get mad, I get even!"?
- Is there some sort of spiritual numbing agent available to dull our pain?
- Are we called to be Christian stoics?
- Are we supposed to "praise the Lord, anyway," acting as though the pain doesn't affect real Christians?
- Should we draw inward, sulk, and mope our way through life?
- Should we complain, "Hey, we don't deserve to be treated like this!"?
- Do we have a right to get even? threaten? slander those who have slandered us?
- Or maybe we should protest, "We won't be doormats anymore!"

Those can be appealing and natural responses when we are suffering unjustly. But they're not Christlike reactions.

When Peter wrote to Christians living with pain and suffering, what kind of hope and direction did the Holy Spirit lead him to give those precious sufferers? Take another look at what Peter wrote in 1 Peter 2:19–23:

> This is a gracious thing, when, mindful of God, one endures sorrows while suffering unjustly. For what credit is it if, when you sin and are beaten for it, you endure? But if when you do good and suffer for it you endure, this is a gracious thing in the sight of God. For to this you have been called, because Christ also suffered for you, leaving you an example, so that you might follow in his steps. He committed no sin, neither was deceit found in his mouth. When he was reviled, he did not revile in return; when he suffered, he did not threaten, but *continued entrusting himself to him who judges justly* [emphasis added].

Comprehending the way Jesus responded to suffering and following in his steps has the potential to revolutionize the way we live in this fallen, painful world.

During our era, between the lost paradise of Eden and the yet-to-be-revealed paradise of the new heaven and the new earth, suffering is a sad reality.

Many of our troubles are the result of our own sinful choices and pursuits. Unlike our Savior, we are not sinless. But at times we undergo physical, emotional, or relational suffering through no fault of our own. We live in a sinful world, daily encountering other sinful people in our communities, workplaces, schools, and even our own homes.

So we need Peter's words that show us God's plan: "To this you have been called, because Christ also suffered for you, leaving you an example, so that you might follow in his steps" (1 Peter 2:21).

The Holy Spirit led the apostle to use a word for *example* that means "copyhead." In that era, when a child was learning to write, the teacher would place at the top of the children's exercise slates the letters or words they were to learn. The teacher required them to carefully copy—to trace—those examples over and over. Using this imagery, Peter says that God wants us to "trace" the example of our suffering Savior.

Contrary to much popular Christianity presented here in the West, Christians are *not* called to live free from pain. In fact, the opposite is true. But our Lord calls us to trace the lifestyle of our suffering leader. We are to "follow in his steps," even as they lead us to become familiar with suffering.

The Source of a Christlike Response

How can we ever endure unjust suffering? How can we respond to the thoughtless employer who makes going to work drudgery instead of joy? How can we take humiliation from a teacher or coach who seems to have it in for us? Or what if our own family members make life painfully difficult through the sinful way they treat us? These are painfully real, crucial questions.

Following in the steps of our Savior means that we, too, "entrust ourselves to him who judges justly."

Like Jesus, we can take our painful situations to our heavenly Father and entrust them—entrust ourselves—to him. And he will give us what we need to deal with them. Then we will find God's promise to the apostle Paul to be true for us, as well. "My grace is sufficient for you, for my power is made perfect in weakness" (2 Corinthians 12:9).

Instead of taking matters into our own hands and seeking retaliation against those who hurt us, God calls us to follow Jesus by responding in faith—faith in our heavenly Father who loves us and will do what is right in his own way and in his own time.

Can we entrust ourselves to our heavenly Father? Absolutely!

Jerry Bridges wrote, "The whole idea of trusting God is, of course, based on the fact that God is absolutely trustworthy."[14] Jesus believed that. He knew that his heavenly Father was trustworthy, so he readily entrusted himself and his suffering "to him who judges justly" (1 Peter 2:23). That is our privilege, too.

Follow in the footsteps of our suffering Savior. Entrust yourself and your suffering to our trustworthy heavenly Father.

- Our Father is omniscient. He knows all about our pain.
- Our Father is omnipotent. He can deal with our suffering.
- Our Father is all wise. He knows the best way to handle our difficulties.
- Our Father is all loving. He cares about us in our trials.
- Entrust yourself to him.

In the true story at the beginning of this chapter, David did not kill King Saul that day. He did not take vengeance on the man who had brought so much suffering into his life. Why did he spare his persecutor? Moments after King Saul left the cave, still unaware of how closely he had come to death, David stepped into the light and called out to Saul, "I have not wronged you, but you are hunting me down to take my life. May the LORD judge between you and me. And may the LORD avenge the wrongs you have done to me, but my hand will not touch you" (1 Samuel 24:11–12). David had taken the pain of unjust suffering and entrusted it—entrusted himself—to his heavenly Father.

Whate'er my God ordains is right:
here shall my stand be taken;
though sorrow, need, or death be mine,
yet I am not forsaken.
My Father's care is round me there;
he holds me that I shall not fall:
and so to Him I leave it all.

—Samuel Rodigast
Translated, Catherine Winkworth

Discussion Questions

SUFFERING LIKE JESUS

1. As you were reading this chapter, what struck you in a fresh way about Jesus' familiarity with suffering?

2. Give some examples of ways we suffer because of our own sinful choices.

3. Discuss some examples of ways we suffer through no fault of our own.

4. What are some common responses to suffering through no fault of our own?

5. When going through difficult times, why do we sometimes struggle with "entrusting ourselves to him who judges justly"?

6. What are some ways we can grow in the ability to entrust God with our pain?

7. Think of some aspect of suffering that is on your heart. Talk to God openly about it. Ask him to help you entrust it to him. "Cast all your anxiety on him because he cares for you" (1 Peter 5:7).

Chapter 9
PERSEVERING LIKE JESUS

IMAGINE THE STARTING LINE OF AN OLYMPIC MARATHON. THE RUNNERS have gathered to begin their race, but one marathoner is wearing a huge backpack, and he's pulling a cart piled high with stuff. He has his cell phone, his earbuds, his digital tablet, his fancy coffee drink— and other things we can't identify, stacked high.

Astonished, we call out, "What are you doing with all that *stuff*?"

"Well," he answers, "I just don't know what I'd do without all my things. I'm taking them along on my marathon today, just in case I might need them."

We would rightly question the sanity of this so-called marathoner. How is he ever going to persevere in this race if he is dragging along all that unnecessary stuff?

The Need for Perseverance

Scripture depicts the Christian life as a race to be run with *perseverance*. It is a marathon, not a sprint. And Hebrews 12:1–2 gives us our race strategy: "Let us also lay aside every weight, and sin which clings so closely, and let us run with endurance the race that is set before us, looking to Jesus, the founder and perfecter of our faith."

Walking like Jesus, day after day, moment by moment, challenges every fiber of our being. But God calls us to persevere for his glory. The Bible gives us numerous examples of people who persevered for God.

1. *Old Testament believers who persevered*. Hebrews 12:1 begins with this phrase: "Therefore, since we are surrounded by such a great cloud of witnesses…" The word *therefore* points back to chapter

eleven—the great "Hall of Faith," that depicts the perseverance of so many Old Testament believers. People such as Noah, Abraham and Sarah, Joseph, Moses, and Rahab testify that the life of faith can indeed be run successfully for God's glory. All these Old Testament believers who persisted through great difficulties now serve as encouraging examples for us.

They are no mere spectators to our race but are experiential witnesses of what can be done through faith in God. These runners have successfully completed the race, and now they testify to us that, by God's grace, we can persevere in running *our* race.

It is as if the crowd of Old Testament saints calls to us from the end point of the course, "Run the race! Don't give up! Run with perseverance! It will be worth it all when you cross the finish line!"

2. *New Testament believers who persevered.* Of all the early followers of Christ who persevered, one stands out:

He sits there shivering. The subterranean dungeon is cold and damp. Paul is lonely. Except for his old friend Luke, everyone has abandoned him. And even though he has not done anything wrong, he is chained like a criminal.

Many of his old friends would have viewed this situation as tragic. Somehow, the brilliant young man had become obsessed with Jesus of Nazareth. He had thrown away a promising future as a Jewish rabbi to become a traveling preacher for this "new religion." Where did it get him? Now an old man, sitting in Rome's Mamertine prison, he awaits his execution. What a shame! What a wasted life!

In the dimly lit dungeon, Paul begins writing something. It is his last letter to his dear "son in the faith," Timothy. Does he complain about his poor living conditions? Is he writing words of despair and regret?

Imagine watching over the apostle Paul's shoulder. He writes, "I am already being poured out as a drink offering, and the time of my departure has come. I have fought the good fight, I have finished the race, I have kept the faith. Henceforth there is laid up for me the crown of righteousness, which the Lord, the righteous judge, will award to me on that day, and not only to me but also to all who have loved his appearing" (2 Timothy 4:6–8).

These are not words of regret but of grateful victory. Paul was about to cross the finish line of his marathon service of Christ. His race had been difficult. He had endured beatings, imprisonment, shipwreck, and abandonment.[15] But, he endured. He *persevered.*

Jesus: The Ultimate Example of Perseverance

In the crowd of those who have already completed the race, one model and motivator of perseverance stands alone: Jesus. Hebrews 12:2 says, "Let us run with endurance the race that is set before us, looking to Jesus."

Good athletes fix their eyes on the goal and never look back—never become distracted by anything off to the side. And God calls us to run our race, undistracted, with our eyes fixed on Jesus.

The author of Hebrews goes on to say that Jesus is the "founder and perfecter" of our faith. Remember: Jesus ran the race, too. He blazed the trail and reached the goal.

He is also the "perfecter" of our faith. He lived his entire earthly life in faithfulness to his heavenly Father. He never got off track. He never quit. He successfully ran the race the Father marked out for him and thus secured our faith. Jesus is our Champion.

Our Savior ran a grueling race of intense physical pain and shame. Deuteronomy 21:23 teaches us, "Anyone who is hung on a tree is under God's curse" (NIV). The cross was a shameful thing. While Jesus was hanging on the cross, God placed all the sins of all his people on his Son's innocent body. Jesus also had to endure the unspeakable pain of his heavenly Father turning his face away. But this was the race marked out for *him.*

Isaiah had prophesied hundreds of years before that the Suffering Servant would be "smitten by God ... afflicted ... pierced ... crushed ... [and wounded]" (53:4–5, brackets added). Still, Jesus *persevered.* He "endured the cross, despising the shame" (Hebrews 12:2). Though his race was immeasurably more difficult than ours, Jesus persevered.

Humanly speaking, Jesus could have quit his race. He could have quit in the wilderness, buckling to the temptations of Satan (Luke 4:1–13). He could have quit in Nazareth the day his neighbors rejected him and sought to kill him (Luke 4:14–30). He could have quit in the garden of Gethsemane, overwhelmed in the anguish of his soul (Matthew 26:36–46).

However, Jesus did not quit. He persevered to the end of his race.

The night before Jesus died on the cross, he prayed to his Father, "I glorified you on earth, having accomplished the work that you gave me to do" (John 17:4). With his dying breath that next day, he cried out in victory, "It is finished!" (John 19:30). And, having finished his race, he took his seat at the right hand of the throne of God (Hebrews 12:2). What a glorious picture of triumphant perseverance!

Our Perseverance

Look at Hebrews 12:1–3 again: "Therefore, since we are surrounded by so great a cloud of witnesses, let us also lay aside every weight, and sin which clings so closely, and let us run with endurance the race that is set before us, looking to Jesus, the founder and perfecter of our faith, who for the joy that was set before him endured the cross, despising the shame, and is seated at the right hand of the throne of God. Consider him who endured from sinners such hostility against himself, so that you may not grow weary or fainthearted."

God calls all of us to persevere in the race, and he has already marked out the course for us. We do not have the liberty to run along whatever course we feel like taking. We need to make sure we are on the right track!

Jesus said, "Enter by the narrow gate. For the gate is wide and the way is easy that leads to destruction, and those who enter by it are many. For the gate is narrow and the way is hard that leads to life, and those who find it are few" (Matthew 7:13–14).

There is only one pathway that leads to eternal life. Jesus proclaimed, "*I am the way*, and the truth, and the life. No one comes to the Father *except through me*" (John 14:6, emphasis added).

So, the first step in running our life marathon is to make sure we are on the right course—the course that leads to eternal life. That means making sure that our hope and trust for eternal life are securely fixed on him, the "founder and perfecter of our faith."

Then God calls us to run our race with perseverance. Apparently, some of the early Jewish Christians (the first recipients of the letter to the Hebrews) had begun their Christian race well but then started to falter. Some wanted to abandon the race Jesus marked out for all of his followers. They wanted to go back to the old track of keeping the Old Testament laws. The author of Hebrews warned them, "Don't do it! Don't get off Jesus' track. Run with endurance. Run with perseverance!"

It takes firm resolve not to drop out of the race—a determination to cross the finish line despite hardship, opposition, exhaustion, and pain. But Jesus himself said, "The one who endures to the end will be saved" (Matthew 10:22).

The Christian life is certainly a challenging marathon, isn't it? What counsel does the Word of God give us for running it successfully?

The author of Hebrews urges us to "lay aside every weight."

Like that would-be marathoner with his heavy backpack and cart full of *stuff,* we can't run a good race if we drag along stuff that only weighs us down. Some of these things may not be sinful in and of themselves, but neither are they helping us run our race. They are excess baggage.

What kinds of things can qualify as excess baggage that hinders us?

1. *Unwise habits.* For example, we all know that scrolling through social media or binge-watching TV or movies can suck up huge portions of time. If they are slowing us down instead of helping us run our race with perseverance, God's Word says to throw off that excess baggage.

2. *Misplaced priorities.* It's common to look back over a week and ask, "Where did all my time go?" We also know that sometimes even "good things" steal our time and attention from God's priorities for us. I'm finding it helpful to add this request to my morning prayers: "Lord, what do you want me *not* to do today?" Such prayers may help us eliminate things that hinder us in running the Christian marathon.

3. *Time-draining possessions and activities.* Most of the things we own today—from our homes to our cars to our electronic devices and

even our pets, require big-time commitments for maintenance. The age-old question is, do we own them, or do they own us?

Our schedules can become similar tyrants. We're pressured to add more and more activities to our already busy lives, which makes running the Christian race more difficult. Often we approach possessions or activities by asking, is this *allowable* for a Christian. Maybe a better question is, will this activity or possession *hinder* me or *help* me in running the race God has marked out for me.

4. *Entangling sins.* Hebrews 12 treats these as a separate category: not just things that hinder us but "sin which clings so closely" (v. 1). In the context of the book of Hebrews, the primary entangling sin is that of unbelief. When we encounter difficulties along the course of life, a lack of faith—a distrust in God's Word—can easily trip us up. We may begin to doubt that following Christ is worth the effort. We may begin to question whether he really cares about our situation. Lack of faith saps spiritual energy right out of us.

Obviously, many other sins can make us stumble as well. Lust for pleasure, power, and possessions can all entangle us as we try to run our race. God tells us to throw off all these entanglements.

John Bunyan, the author of the classic *Pilgrim's Progress*, advised Christians to turn a deaf ear when the sins of the world call to us, seeking to distract us and get us off course: "Let me alone…come not nigh [near] me, for I am running for heaven…. If I win, I win all, and if I lose, I lose all; let me alone, for I will not hear!"[16]

Our race may be difficult, but God wants our commitment to *persevere*. What encouragements does he provide to help us keep going?

Start paying attention to the stories of many other believers in Scripture—and throughout the centuries since—who have successfully stayed the course and completed their races. This great cloud of witnesses reminds us that God is faithful, and he will enable us to finish the race.

But above all other encouragements to endure is the confidence we gain by fixing our eyes on Jesus, "the founder and perfecter of our faith." Jesus fixed his eyes on the goal set before him: redeeming his people from their sin. That was the "joy that was set before him." To reach that goal, he had to endure the cross, but he persevered. And now he is seated at the right hand of God. (See Hebrews 12:2.)

Because Jesus completed his race, he enables us to complete ours. "Consider him who endured from sinners such hostility against himself, so that you may not grow weary or fainthearted" (Hebrews 12:3). Letting go of what hinders us and firmly fixing our eyes on our Savior, we can persevere in the race he has marked out for us.

> Through many dangers, toils and snares,
> I have already come;
> 'Tis grace has brought me safe thus far,
> And grace will lead me home.
> And when this flesh and heart shall fail;
> And mortal life shall cease,
> I shall possess within the veil
> A life of joy and peace.

—John Newton

Discussion Questions
PERSEVERING LIKE JESUS

1. Since our goal is to successfully finish the marathon of the Christian life, what are some practical ways to keep this goal in view, day by day?

2. Consider the "stuff" of your life. What excess baggage (in the form of bad habits, wrong priorities, or lack of faith) is slowing you down as you run the race? What do you believe God is calling you to do with the stuff that is hindering you in your Christian life?

3. What might be some indicators that a Christian friend is beginning to waver in his or her commitment to persevere? Read Hebrews 3:12–14 as you prayerfully consider your ministry to this wavering friend.

4. Who is one of your favorite Bible characters who persevered in his or her commitment to the Lord? What is there about his or her life that encourages you to persevere in your own Christian race?

5. How can our churches more faithfully encourage a long-range view of the Christian life—that it's not a sprint but a marathon that requires perseverance to the end?

6. This week, spend some time with God, asking him to point out to you any specific hindrances or sinful entanglements that are slowing you down in your spiritual progress. Ask the Lord to help you throw them off so you will "not grow weary and lose heart."

Chapter 10

PRACTICING PATIENCE LIKE JESUS

THEY KILLED STEPHEN THAT DAY. FILLED WITH THE HOLY SPIRIT, STEphen had preached powerfully of Jesus Christ as Lord and Savior. The religious establishment grew furious. So they dragged Stephen outside the city walls of Jerusalem and threw rocks at him until his body lay dead beside the road—bloodied and broken. "And Saul was there, giving approval to his death" (Acts 8:1 NIV).

That's how we meet this promising young rabbi known as Saul of Tarsus. He was standing there near the dead body of Stephen, probably with a smug smile because now this preaching deacon would no longer be speaking of Jesus Christ.

Acts 8 and 9 add more dark colors to Saul's portrait. After godly men mourned deeply for Stephen, Saul made it his mission to destroy all followers of Christ, wherever he could find them. Trekking from house to house, he dragged off both men and women and threw them in prison for their heretical beliefs (from Saul's point of view).

The portrait grows darker still. Saul threatened to murder all the Lord's disciples. He even asked for, and received, written permission from the high priest to go to the Damascus synagogues and hunt down any men and women who belonged to "the Way" and haul them off to prison in Jerusalem.

This picture of Saul of Tarsus is not one conjured up by those who had a vendetta against him. By his own mouth he would later confess, "I myself was convinced that I ought to do many things in opposing the name of Jesus of Nazareth." (See Acts 26:9–11.)

Would you want this man living in your neighborhood? Saul had an obsessive hatred of Jesus Christ and everyone who followed him. Whether you were a man or a woman, he would travel great distances to arrest you and throw you into prison. He would do whatever he could to force you to recant your faith in Jesus Christ. And, if the court were deciding whether you should live or die, he would vote for the death sentence every time.

Here's a question worth pondering: Why didn't Jesus stop him from destroying the lives of those precious believers?

Jesus *did* stop him one day. Saul (now Paul) describes the day he encountered Jesus Christ. "In this connection I journeyed to Damascus with the authority and commission of the chief priests. At midday... I saw on the way a light from heaven, brighter than the sun, that shone around me and those who journeyed with me. And when we had all fallen to the ground, I heard a voice saying to me in the Hebrew language, 'Saul, Saul, why are you persecuting me?'" (Acts 26:12–14).

Is Jesus finally going to stomp on this proud Pharisee assassin like a cockroach?

Paul asked who was calling him.

"I am Jesus, whom you are persecuting," the Lord replied. "But rise and stand upon your feet, for I have appeared to you for this purpose, to appoint you as a servant and witness to the things in which you have seen me and to those in which I will appear to you, delivering you from your people and from the Gentiles—to whom I am sending you to open their eyes, so that they may turn from darkness to light and from the power of Satan to God, that they may receive forgiveness of sins and a place among those who are sanctified by faith in me" (Acts 26:15–18).

Did you catch that? Instead of crushing this man obsessed with destroying the church, Jesus is going to make him a missionary! Why would Jesus do that? Thought-provoking question, isn't it? Why would Jesus tolerate this violent, callous, self-righteous, bigoted persecutor of the church for so long, and then finally intervene—not to stomp him out—but to save him and make him a missionary of the gospel?

Jesus, the Ultimate Model of Patience

The answer centers on the person of Jesus Christ. Paul wrote this explanation to his protégé, Timothy: "The saying is trustworthy and deserving of full acceptance, that Christ Jesus came into the world to save sinners, of whom I am the foremost. But I received mercy for this reason, that in me, as the foremost, Jesus Christ might display his perfect patience as an example to those who were to believe in him for eternal life" (1 Timothy 1:15–16).

Twice in that paragraph to Timothy, Paul referred to himself as the worst of sinners. No doubt many people today read that self-assessment and think, "Oh, come on Paul. You're just trying to be humble. You weren't that bad. Lots of people were worse sinners than you!"

But why try to talk Paul out of this self-assessment? In that same letter to Timothy, he said he had been a blasphemer, a persecutor, and a violent man (v. 13).

Paul (then named Saul) really had been guilty of blaspheming the name of Christ, persecuting the believers purchased with the blood of Jesus, and committing great violence against the precious sons and daughters of the High King of heaven.

I wonder if Paul had nightmares about his past sins against Christ and his church. I wonder if he could see the bloody, broken body of Stephen lying there along the road. I wonder if he could hear the sound of children crying as he hauled their parents off to jail. Paul considered himself the worst of sinners, and it's as if he were saying, "If you were to line up all the sinners of the world in order of the magnitude of their offenses, I would be in the front row!"

Yet how did Jesus treat the self-confessed "foremost sinner?" Paul said, "The grace of our Lord overflowed for me" (v. 14). That day on the road near Damascus, in the very midst of all the obsessive violence against Christians, Saul of Tarsus was saved by the amazing, sovereign grace and mercy of Jesus Christ.

Astonishingly, Jesus not only saved this persecutor from the hell he deserved, but he also transformed him into a highly effective instrument in spreading the gospel (v. 12). I wonder if, after a long day of ministry, Paul might have lain on his bed at night with tears of astonished gratitude wetting his pillow. I wonder if he might have prayed something like this:

> Dear Jesus, thank you so much for taking this mouth that used to blaspheme your holy name—breathing out murderous threats—and filling it with sweet messages of your grace. Thank you for taking this hard and hateful heart that was so full of animosity toward you and your precious children and filling it with a passion to know you and to love your dear people. Thank you, dear Jesus, for taking this proud Pharisee, so bent on destroying your church, and using me to build up your kingdom all over the world. Your grace is so amazing, precious Jesus. I love you. Amen.

So, why, despite Saul's obsessive hatred and horrific actions, did Jesus show him mercy and grace? Jesus' reason focused not so much on Saul, the receiver of grace, as it did on Jesus himself, the giver of grace.

In Saul, the worst of sinners, Jesus put on display one of his amazing attributes—his patience. Instead of crushing this murderous persecutor, Jesus tolerated him day after painful day, week after painful week, month after painful month. And then, one day, wonder of wonders, Jesus poured out his mercy and grace, changing Saul's whole life and even his name.

Jesus' Patience on Display

Paul was not an exceptional case. In fact, the Bible says he was an example—a prototype—of the kind of people Jesus chooses to save in order to put his amazing patience on display.

1. *Jesus' amazing display of patience with Saul.* He chose to save Saul (Paul) to show what he can do in anyone who believes in him and receives eternal life (1 Timothy 1:16).

This is such an important truth that it became a "trustworthy saying" in the early church: "Christ Jesus came into the world to save sinners" (v. 15).

2. *Jesus' amazing display of patience with us in salvation.* We, as Christians, may look back at our life before Christ saved us and ask, "Why

didn't the Lord crush me for all those years I sinned against him?" Or "Why did he choose to save me while young, preserving me from those serious wrong turns I surely would have taken?"

The apostle Peter explained it this way: "The Lord is…patient toward you, not wishing that any should perish, but that all should reach repentance" (2 Peter 3:9), and "Bear in mind that our Lord's patience means salvation" (2 Peter 3:15 NIV).

If you are a true follower of Jesus Christ, your life serves as a canvas on which Jesus has painted a portrait of his own character—including this attribute of patience.

3. *Jesus' amazing display of patience in us every day.* Our Lord continues to show mercy when we sin. Charles Spurgeon wrote, "It is a great act of eternal love when Christ once for all absolves the sinner and puts him into the family of God; but what condescending patience there is when the Saviour with much long-suffering bears the oft recurring follies of his wayward disciple; day by day, and hour by hour, washing away the multiplied transgressions of his erring but beloved child! To dry up a flood of rebellion is something marvelous, but to endure the constant dropping of repeated offences–to bear with a perpetual trying of patience, this is love indeed!"[17]

Jesus' Patience, Our Model for Relationships

God calls us to mirror the gracious patience Jesus has shown us. But daily irritations often challenge our patience:

- the inconsiderate driver who cuts us off
- the person near us in the restaurant, conversing loudly on her cell phone
- the rude cashier at the checkout line
- our noisy children (or someone else's)
- our sulking teen
- our forgetful elderly relative
- our spouse who sees an issue differently.

Sometimes it's difficult to treat friends and family members with the patience Christ has shown us less-than-ideal children of God.

I remember a time when my wife had locked her keys in her car—again. (I share this story with her permission.) She called and asked me if I could come rescue her. I agreed, but let's just say I was less than happy to abruptly leave my breakfast meeting. During my ten-minute drive to help her, the Holy Spirit prodded my stubborn, impatient heart. I can't recall what I was muttering under my breath for those first few minutes. But, in his grace, the Lord reminded me how patient he has been with me over the years. By the time I pulled my car next to my wife's, the Holy Spirit's fruit of patience (Galatians 5:22) was starting to bud in my heart.

How can we better reflect our Lord's patience wherever we are?

Remembering the patience Christ continually shows us, maybe we can show more patience toward that demanding boss who piles on the work. The teacher who shows little sympathy to the struggling student. The coworkers who aren't pulling their share of the load.

Remembering the patience Christ continually shows us, maybe we can show more patience toward our fellow church members: That person who talks too much in our Sunday School class or small group. That church member whose preferred worship style is so different from our own. That board member who says, "But we've never done that before."

Remembering the patience Christ continually shows us, maybe we can even show more patience toward our Lord. He wants us to develop a confident patience as we take our concerns to him, day after day, month after month, year after year without any apparent answers to our requests.

Oh, how patient Jesus was with the worst of sinners! How patient he has been with you and me! May we be grateful reflectors of his patience.

Paul urges us, "Walk in a manner worthy of the calling to which you have been called, with all humility and gentleness, with patience, bearing with one another in love" (Ephesians 4:1–2).

Perhaps you would join me in praying this prayer: Dear Lord, I cannot comprehend how you could be so patient with me. I have often ignored you, disobeyed you, and placed you on the periphery of my life. Thank you for not treating me as my sins deserve but showing me your saving and cleansing patience. Help me reflect to the people I encounter every day the patience you have shown me.

Patience! O what grace divine!
Given by the God of love and power,
That leans upon a father's hand,
In every dark, afflicting hour.

—Thomas Gibbons

Discussion Questions

PRACTICING PATIENCE LIKE JESUS

1. How did Jesus show his patience with you before you were saved?

2. Why did Jesus save you? Which of his attributes does he put on display when he saves undeserving sinners like you and me?

3. In what situations do you most often show impatience?

4. How does Christ's patience toward you impact how you treat other people who try your patience?

5. Think right now of one or two people with whom you find it especially difficult to be patient. Pray for God's blessing upon them. Ask God to give you opportunities to show Christlike patience to them.

Chapter 11
FORGIVING LIKE JESUS

Have you ever wondered what was going through the minds of the Roman soldiers standing guard at that horrible place of Jesus' crucifixion? At times, veteran soldiers no doubt had heard loud curses of enraged criminals being executed. Other times, pitiful cries for mercy escaped the convicts' lips.

But never had they heard anything like these words of Jesus: "Father, forgive them, for they know not what they do" (Luke 23:34).

What might the Jewish religious leaders have been thinking? Some of them had come outside Jerusalem's walls to make sure this troublemaker got his due. Did assured smirks suddenly turn to confused frowns as they heard this unexpected prayer? They had fiendishly manipulated his execution. How could he pray, "Father, *forgive* them"?

What is forgiveness anyway? Forgiveness, in a Christian context, is the choice to surrender to Christ our resentment, anger, or desire to punish or get even with those who have hurt us. The most common word for *forgiveness* in the original language of the New Testament conveys this idea of "letting go."

Whom Did Jesus Forgive?

The Gospels relate many stories of people to whom Jesus gave his grace-filled forgiveness:

1. *Jesus forgave repentant sinners.* Jesus forgave people who were truly sorry—people who repented of their sins. You may remember the Bible's story of the woman heartbroken over her sinful life.

When she heard that Jesus was eating at the home of her Pharisee neighbor, she made her way over to that house and brought with her an expensive alabaster jar of perfume, likely her most treasured possession. Perhaps she had heard Jesus talking about God's forgiveness and had taken it to heart. Overwhelmed with grief and regret, she stood behind him as he reclined at the table and ate. Tears ran down her cheeks and splashed onto his feet. Then, after kneeling and wiping off the tears with her long hair, she kissed his feet and poured her precious perfume on them. (See Luke 7:37–38.)

Although this woman was devastated over her sin, the religious leaders of Jesus' day still looked on her with disdain. But how did Jesus see her? He said, "Your sins are forgiven" (v. 48). Jesus freely forgave *repentant sinners*.

2. *Jesus forgave his enemies.* Jesus even forgave people who were not sorry for their sins—those who had not even asked for forgiveness. As Jesus was being nailed to the cross, his first utterance was the astonishing "Father, forgive them." To whom was Jesus referring when he said *them*? On whose behalf did Jesus ask his Father' forgiveness?

- The Jewish leaders. Jesus was asking the Father to forgive the very people who had twisted his teaching, slandered his character, and insisted upon his crucifixion.

- The Roman soldiers. Jesus also was asking the Father to forgive the Roman soldiers who had so horribly abused him with rods, whips, fists, and the crown of thorns. It was the Roman soldiers who had beaten Jesus' body into a bloody pulp. It was the Roman soldiers who had pounded those spikes through his hands and feet. And now it was those Roman soldiers Jesus was asking God to forgive.

- The crowd. At the foot of the cross a crowd had gathered, gawking at our precious, agonizing Savior. During the very time the jeering spectators were spewing out words of hatred and mockery, Jesus was asking his heavenly Father to forgive them.

From a human standpoint we might have expected Jesus' prayer regarding these enemies to be something like, "Father, make them stop hurting me! I don't deserve this abuse! Pour out your wrath on these people who are torturing and mocking me! Send your judgment on these crucifiers!"

But instead, we hear the Savior pray, "Father, forgive them." Isn't that amazing?

Sometimes we have difficulty forgiving people who ask us for forgiveness. Sometimes we withhold forgiveness even from people who are truly sorry for how they have hurt us. But we see Jesus forgiving his abusers while they were in the process of murdering him! They were not broken over their sin. They were not asking for forgiveness. Yet Jesus prayed for his Father to forgive them. The prophecy of Isaiah 53:12 takes on flesh: "Yet he bore the sin of many, and makes intercession for the transgressors."

Why Was Jesus So Forgiving?

The answer to this *why* question is not found in the people he forgave. They certainly did not deserve his forgiveness. The answer is in Jesus himself.

1. *Jesus' forgiveness reflected his Father's character.* He was on mission to show us the character of God the Father. And the Father is a forgiving God.

In Psalm 103:8–12 King David wrote,

The LORD is merciful and gracious,
    slow to anger and abounding in steadfast love.
He will not always chide,
    nor will he keep his anger forever.
He does not deal with us according to our sins,
    nor repay us according to our iniquities.
For as high as the heavens are above the earth,
    so great is his steadfast love toward those who fear him;
as far as the east is from the west,
    so far does he remove our transgressions from us.

Jesus, God's precious Son, was the "exact representation" here on earth of this forgiving God (Hebrews 1:3 NIV).

2. *Jesus' forgiveness provided for the salvation of sinners.* Jesus also forgave in order to fulfill another of his purposes in coming to this sinful earth. In the previous chapter we saw Paul's proclamation:

"Christ Jesus came into the world to save sinners" (1 Timothy 1:15). All of us who are the undeserving recipients of that forgiveness are eternally grateful.

Why Should We Forgive Those Who Hurt Us?

In our quest throughout this book, we have found that as Christians, our guide for daily living is this: "Whoever says he abides in him ought to walk in the same way in which he walked" (1 John 2:5–6). How does his forgiveness impact daily life in our homes, schools, jobs, churches, and communities?

1. *God calls us to forgive others because he has forgiven us.* The basis for forgiving other people is not the way they treat us but the way Christ has already treated us. He forgave our innumerable offenses. So, standing on the sure footing of his forgiveness, we can then forgive those who hurt us.

You may be thinking, "But you don't know how that person hurt me! You don't know the deep pain and scars I carry because of it. They don't *deserve* to be forgiven! Why should I forgive someone who has hurt me so?"

That is a common human reaction. Often, we withhold forgiveness, justifying our stubbornness with "She doesn't deserve to be forgiven because of how badly she hurt me. There's no way I could forgive her after what she did to me!"

This kind of response approaches the problem from the wrong direction. Our forgiveness is not based on the offender's worthiness. We forgive because we have been forgiven. The apostle Paul wrote, "Be kind to one another, tenderhearted, forgiving one another, as God in Christ forgave you" (Ephesians 4:32).

Forgiven sinners forgive sinners.

Paul also urges us to bear with one another, and "if one has a compaint against another, forgiving each other; *as the Lord has forgiven you, so you also must forgive*" (Colossians 3:13, emphasis added). There is no room for bitterness in our hearts if we're following the forgiving Jesus Christ. There is no place for grudges, no justification for getting even.

Because we have personally experienced the astonishing forgiveness of Christ, he calls us to forgive—not only those who ask our forgiveness, but, like our Lord, also those who hurt us and never seek forgiveness. Jesus clearly said, "Love your enemies and pray for those who persecute you" (Matthew 5:44).

Many people have been gripped by the story of Louis Zamperini, powerfully portrayed in the book and movie titled *Unbroken*. As a prisoner of war in Japan during World War II, Zamperini was singled out for brutal torture by a seemingly demented Japanese guard nicknamed *The Bird*.

Some years after the war, Zamperini returned to the place of his nightmares, seeking out the guards who tormented him. In particular, Zamperini wanted to find The Bird. Why? To offer his forgiveness. When astonished onlookers asked him how he could forgive this twisted, sadistic guard, Zamperini relayed the story of how Christ had forgiven Zamperini himself. It was the forgiveness he had experienced in Christ that had moved him to forgive The Bird.

May the forgiveness each of us has received through Christ motivate us to forgive those who have hurt us. We forgive because we have been forgiven, not because the person who brought us such pain and grief deserves it.

2. *God calls us to forgive others because we want to be forgiven.* Jesus taught, "If you forgive others their trespasses, your heavenly Father will also forgive you, but if you do not forgive others their trespasses, neither will your Father forgive your trespasses" (Matthew 6:14–15). Would we want Jesus to forgive us only as much as we have forgiven those who have sinned against us?

Jesus illustrated this point for his Galilean listeners with the parable of the unmerciful servant. The apostle Matthew recorded the story in Matthew 18:32–35.

A king's servant could not pay a large debt he owed his master. The king took pity on the man and forgave his unpayable debt. Sadly, this same servant refused to forgive a much smaller debt owed by a fellow servant. When the king heard about such hard-heartedness, he called him a wicked servant. "I forgave you all that debt because you pleaded with me. And should not you have had mercy on your fellow servant, as I had mercy on you?" (vv. 32–33).

93

The king was so angry he sentenced the servant to be tortured in prison until he paid back everything he owed the king.

Jesus concluded his story with this sobering application: "So also my heavenly Father will do to every one of you, if you do not forgive your brother from your heart."

How Can We Become More Forgiving?

Acknowledging that forgiveness goes against our human nature, how *can* we walk like Jesus in forgiveness?

1. *By remembering who our heavenly Father is.* He knows all about our situations, and he will deal with them in his time and in his way. Often, when we take vengeance, we are, in essence, protesting, "God, I don't like the way you are handling this injustice. That person hurt me, and you are not doing anything about it. I'm taking matters into my own hands!"

Can we trust God to take care of the offenses other people commit against us? Do we trust him to take care of our pain? We can, considering all we have been learning about his character.

So consider the apostle Paul's admonition in Romans 12:17–19: "Do not repay anyone evil for evil. Be careful to do what is right in the eyes of everyone. If it is possible, as far as it depends on you, live at peace with everyone. Do not take revenge, my friends, but leave room for God's wrath, for it is written: 'It is mine to avenge; I will repay,' says the Lord" (NIV).

2. *By remembering whose we are.* We are God's forgiven children. He has shown us amazing grace in granting us forgiveness even though we have offended him time and again. Can't we forgive the lesser sins other people commit against us? God has treated us with grace, mercy, and forgiveness. How can we treat others with bitterness, vengeance, and unforgiveness?

Jesus said that from those who have received much, much will be required (Luke 12:48). We could paraphrase that in this context: "He who has been forgiven much, is required to forgive much."

3. *By deliberately choosing to show compassion to those who have hurt us.* Romans 12:20–21 commands this humanly unnatural response: "'If

your enemy is hungry, feed him; if he is thirsty, give him something to drink; for by so doing you will heap burning coals on his head.' Do not be overcome by evil, but overcome evil with good."

Many Christians, as they have obeyed this directive from Romans 12, can testify how the Lord softened their hearts toward those who have hurt them. Showing compassion often changes the heart of the offended, making it easier to lovingly forgive the offender.

A lady came to her pastor and his wife, pouring out the pain and anger in her heart against her husband's broken marriage vows. Bitterness over her husband's betrayal was clearly eating her up inside. As the pastoral couple listened with compassion, they eventually suggested she begin to pray for her husband—that he would be broken over his sin and seek the Lord's forgiveness.

Though hard at first, she agreed, and over time, her bitterness gave way to unexpected compassion for the man who had brought such grief into her life. She found herself moved to do small acts of kindness for her estranged husband—sending him notes indicating that she was praying for him and inviting him to their children's school events.

Some months later, the Lord answered her prayers, and her repentant husband came humbly seeking her forgiveness. By then, the Lord had softened her heart, enabling her to forgive her husband even as Christ had forgiven her.

Every follower of Jesus has been, and will be, hurt by other people. Let go of all bitterness, forgive as you have been forgiven. And put that forgiveness to work through acts of compassion.

In wonder lost, with trembling joy,
We take the pardon of our God:
Pardon for crimes of deepest dye,
A pardon bought with Jesus' blood,
A pardon bought with Jesus' blood.
Who is a pardoning God like Thee?
Or who has grace so rich and free?
Or who has grace so rich and free?
Great God of wonders!

—Samuel Davies

Discussion Questions

FORGIVING LIKE JESUS

1. What is a good definition of forgiveness?

2. Why is it so difficult to forgive those who hurt us?

3. Why should we forgive those who hurt us or sin against us? See Colossians 3:13 and Ephesians 4:32.

4. How does our willingness to forgive others impact what we should expect on judgment day? Carefully read Matthew 6:14–15 before answering.

5. Read Romans 12:17–19. There is only one seat behind the bench of the great Judge of all the universe. Who is sitting on it? What are we saying about our view of God when we seek retribution instead of offering forgiveness to others?

6. Think of someone who has hurt you. In what tangible ways can you demonstrate that you have forgiven him or her? Discuss some specific acts of compassion you could do for that person. Choose one and do it this week.

Chapter 12
PRAYING LIKE JESUS

VERY EARLY IN THE MORNING, SIMON PETER'S HOUSE GUEST GOT UP QUIetly and slipped into the cool, still-dark streets of the lakeside town of Capernaum. Making his way along the deserted lanes, he left the town and found a place where he could be alone. However, he was not really alone because he spent those precious hours conversing with his heavenly Father.

Suddenly a concerned Peter and friends interrupted Jesus. We can imagine their exasperation. "Where have you been?" they cried. "We've been looking for you everywhere!" (See Mark 1:35–37.)

What Was Jesus' Prayer Life Like?

Have you ever noticed that Jesus prayed a lot? James Stewart, professor of New Testament at Edinburgh University, wrote, "Prayer was the habitual atmosphere of Jesus' daily life."[18]

We can learn much from Scripture about our Lord's prayer life.

1. *Jesus prayed often.* The Gospel writers record many accounts of Jesus praying. And no doubt he prayed countless other times than those the writers witnessed and recorded.

Consider some of the occasions on which Jesus prayed:

• He prayed at his baptism, beginning his public ministry (Luke 3:21).

• He prayed before a busy day of serving others (Mark 1:35–39).

• He prayed at the end of a full day of ministry and miracles (Luke 5:15–16).

97

- He prayed before making major decisions, such as choosing the twelve apostles (Luke 6:12).
- He prayed in his last few hours with his disciples (John17).
- He prayed the night before he went to the cross–during the time of his most severe trial in the garden of Gethsemane (Luke 22:39–46).
- He prayed during the unfathomable anguish of the cross. Jesus died praying (Luke 23:34, 46).

Unlike many, Jesus prayed not only when people were watching and listening, but also when no one else would have noticed. Luke tells us, "He would withdraw to desolate places and pray" (Luke 5:16). He prayed when his only audience was the One who truly mattered—his heavenly Father.

2. *Jesus prayed passionately.* Prayer was no meaningless ritual for Jesus. Luke described Jesus' Gethsemane prayer this way: "Being in agony he prayed more earnestly; and his sweat became like great drops of blood falling down to the ground" (Luke 22:44). The author of Hebrews wrote, "He offered up prayers and petitions with loud cries and tears" (5:7).

3. *Jesus prayed urgently.* Jesus seemed compelled to pray. Sometimes he would get up at 3:00 or 4:00 in the morning to talk with his heavenly Father (see Mark 1:35, for example). Even though Jesus led a very busy life, with many people making demands on his time, Jesus made time to pray.

4. *Jesus prayed at length.* At times Jesus offered up short prayers, but on other occasions he prayed for hours. In fact, Luke wrote about one occasion when Jesus "went out to the mountain to pray, and all night he continued in prayer to God" (Luke 6:12).

Why Did Jesus Pray?

Nineteenth century Scottish theologian William Blaikie observed something that no doubt many readers of the Gospel accounts have considered: "Beautiful though the prayerfulness of Jesus be in itself, yet when we think of who he was, it takes us somewhat by surprise."[19]

Similarly, his contemporary, American theologian John Broadus, wrote, "If any human being was ever able to stand alone in the universe, without leaning on God, it might have been true of [Jesus]."[20]

Yes, we might assume that Jesus did not need to pray. Yet prayerfulness marked his life. So why did Jesus pray?

1. *Jesus* wanted *to pray.* He said, "The Father loves the Son" (John 5:20). And, fully assured of his Father's love, Jesus, in turn, loved his Father. Jesus sometimes prayed purely to enjoy communion with his heavenly Father who "loved [him] before the foundation of the world" (John 17:24). At those times, Jesus was not talking to his Father because he needed something. He simply wanted to talk to his Father who loved him.

What kind of son would talk to his father only when he wanted something? A loving son would chat with his father for the pure enjoyment of their personal relationship. We may assume Jesus never wanted to be isolated from his much-loved Father, so he sought opportunities, day and night, to talk to him.

2. *Jesus* needed *to pray.* Thoughtfully read Hebrews 5:7: "In the days of his flesh, Jesus offered up prayers and supplications, with loud cries and tears, to him who was able to save him from death." In other words, Jesus prayed because he was a man—a real human being. J. Oswald Sanders wrote, "Though truly divine, His deity in no way affected the reality of His human nature. His prayers were as real and intense as any ever offered."[21]

In other words, Jesus prayed because, as a human being, he was aware of his dependence on his heavenly Father. He needed wisdom in decision making, so he went to his heavenly Father to request it. He needed strength while working miracles and resisting Satan's attacks. So he asked for it.

Jesus' amazing power and wisdom during his earthly ministry clearly came from his dependence on his heavenly Father. Jesus came to the only true Source to be supplied with everything he needed. Jesus prayed not only because he *wanted* to, but also because he *needed* to.

Commands and Hindrances

How can our prayer lives reflect that of our Master's? We have a number of scriptural commands:

- "Be ... constant in prayer" (Romans 12:12).
- "Praying at all times in the Spirit" (Ephesians 6:18).
- "Continue steadfastly in prayer" (Colossians 4:2).
- "Pray without ceasing, give thanks in all circumstances; for this is the will of God in Christ Jesus for you" (1 Thessalonians 5:17–18).

But an honest assessment may point out some of our deficiencies:

1. *Seldom praying when others aren't watching or listening.* Jesus gives us a direct command: "When you pray, go into your room and shut the door and pray to your Father who is in secret. And your Father who sees in secret will reward you" (Matthew 6:6). Charles Spurgeon, the nineteenth century pastor of Metropolitan Tabernacle in London, once charged in a sermon, "If you do not pray alone, you do not pray at all."[22]

2. *Infrequent or anemic prayers.* Jesus, our example, prayed, often, privately, passionately, urgently, and sometimes at length. Devotional writer Andrew Murray wrote, "In His life of secret prayer, my Savior is my example."[23] If we are committed to "walking like Jesus," why is it so difficult to maintain a prayer life like his?

3. *Overly busy schedules.* We may say, I'm just so busy! Yet Jesus often had extremely full days too—preaching, teaching, working miracles, and traveling. Our days are often jammed full, but his were even more so. The busyness excuse becomes indefensible because Jesus' overflowing days became a *reason* to pray, not an excuse to skip it.

Our prayerlessness may be a symptom of a deeper problem. To truly evaluate our own prayerlessness, it would be wise (though perhaps painful) to review Jesus' reasons for leading a life of prayerfulness.

Jesus talked with his heavenly Father because he wanted to. So our own prayerlessness may reveal *a lack of desire* to pray—with excuses such as I really don't feel like it, or I just don't want to pray right now.

Jesus talked with his heavenly Father because of their close relationship. If we are praying little, perhaps our love for God has grown cool and our confidence in his love for us is waning. A lack of communication with God is a sign that the relationship has grown distant, much like the sad relationship of a married couple who rarely have meaningful conversations.

Prayerlessness may indicate a growing distance from the God who bought us with the blood of his precious Son. The times we don't feel like praying are often the times we most *need* to pray! Drawing closer to our Father warms our relationship once again. God invites us to confidently "draw near to the throne of grace, that we may receive mercy and find grace to help in time of need" (Hebrews 4:16).

Jesus talked with his heavenly Father because he needed to. What does that tell us about our lack of prayer? Do we think we *don't* need to pray—that we can get along fine without God's help? Prayerlessness may be a symptom of our pride—a vain assumption of self-sufficiency. But if Jesus needed to consult his heavenly Father while here on earth, how much more do we?

Prayerlessness is not a small problem. It rarely stems from mere busyness or weariness or lack of discipline. More often, we don't pray because we don't *want* to pray or we think we *don't need to* pray.

Prayerlessness reveals a problem with our core beliefs and values. Pride and self-sufficiency lay at the heart of sin—including the sin of prayerlessness.

Mirroring Jesus' Prayer Life

So what can we do to walk like Jesus in the area of our prayers?

1. *Confess.* Agree with God about what prayerlessness is: sin. It is disobedience to Scripture's commands to pray, and it is totally unlike our Savior's example. Only in coming into the presence of the King of the Universe can we see our pride as a treasonous attempt to be our own "gods"—to control our own worlds. How ugly. How sinful. But oh, what a comfort it is to know that "If we confess our sins, he is faithful and just to forgive us our sins and to cleanse us from all unrighteousness" (1 John 1:9).

2. *Repent.* Only a change of thinking leads to a genuine change of daily life.

101

Instead of thinking this:
    I can get along without God on this one,
pray this:
    Oh, Lord, how I need you. I can do nothing without you!

Instead of thinking this:
    I can figure things out on my own,
remember this pride-eradicating question that God asked Job:
    "Where were you when I laid the foundation of the earth?"
    (Job 38:4).

Instead of thinking this:
    I'm self-sufficient. I've got this covered,
remember this:
    "What do you have that you did not receive?"
    (1 Corinthians 4:7).

Instead of thinking this:
    I need what the world offers to meet my needs,
remember this:
    "Every good gift and every perfect gift is from above"
    (James 1:17).

3. *Pray.* Make the time. Walking like Jesus means living a life marked by prayers—private, passionate, urgent, and even, at times, lengthy prayer. How much more brightly could we reflect Christ in our dark world if, like him, we spent more time in prayer? *"Lord, teach us to pray!"*

Arise, my soul, arise;
shake off thy guilty fears;
The bleeding Sacrifice
in my behalf appears:
Before the Throne my surety stands.
My name is written on His hands.

My God is reconciled;
His pardoning voice I hear;
He owns me for his child,
I can no longer fear:

With confidence I now draw nigh,
And "Father, Abba, Father," cry.

—Charles Wesley

Discussion Questions

PRAYING LIKE JESUS

1. What characteristics of Jesus' prayer life especially challenge you? Why?

2. Identify the two key reasons Jesus prayed as noted in this chapter.

3. What are some common reasons Christians give for not praying? Which of these are legitimate reasons?

4. Describe what you would like your prayer life to be like.

5. List some ways you think your church could encourage church members to grow in their prayer lives. How could you serve your church in encouraging this?

6. If you are married or living in a family context, list some ways you can improve your prayer times as a couple or family?

7. If you are not currently doing so, choose a time and place for praying to God daily. Share that commitment with one or two family members or close friends.

Chapter 13
SERVING LIKE JESUS

THE SUN WAS SETTING AS THE MEN GATHERED FOR THE PASSOVER MEAL. Many things about the evening were familiar to these Jewish men. They found comfort in the familiarity of the Passover elements and liturgy with which they had all grown up. On the table were the lamb, the unleavened bread, the wine, and the bitter herbs. Yet, mixed with the comfort of the familiar, an uneasiness marked that spring evening. Whispers floated back and forth among the men gathered for the meal. There was talk of betrayal.

There was also a socially awkward realization that no one had yet performed that common act of hospitality—washing the guests' feet. Off to the side of that upper room sat a pitcher and basin next to a long linen towel. Everyone knew the function of those household items. The walk from Bethany had been dusty for Jesus and these twelve followers. Someone should get up and wash the feet of those present. But who?

Maybe ambitious Peter would pop up and volunteer. Or maybe one of the strong silent types, like Andrew the fisherman. Then again, maybe John. After all, he was the youngest. The meal continued in awkwardness, with an undercurrent of a debate. Luke later recorded that they were arguing about which of them was the greatest (Luke 22:24).

Suddenly, without comment, the Master himself stood and took off his outer clothing. Wrapping the long linen towel around his waist, Jesus suddenly looked like a common slave. Then, bringing pitcher and basin, the Master knelt and worked his way around the table, washing and drying the feet of his followers, man by man.

The apostle John set the scene with this background: Jesus knew "that the Father had given all things into his hands, and that he had come from God and was going back to God" (John 13:3).

What was John's point? Jesus was not operating out of a position of weakness but of power. Not out of a position of insecurity but of certainty. Secure in his relationship with his heavenly Father, he was confident he would soon return to his place of honor and glory.

Our Savior knew that the Father had put all things "into his hands." So what did Jesus do? He didn't demand to be served by his followers. He served them, doing the most menial of jobs—despite their prideful debate and neglect in serving one another.

Jesus, Our Model of Servanthood

Jesus acted purposefully in everything he did. And he took advantage of teachable moments. As this story continues, we can see a couple things he was teaching them in this situation:

1. *Jesus was teaching the disciples that they needed him to cleanse them.* Peter, the outspoken disciple so many of us relate to, protested the incongruity of his Lord's action. "Never!" Peter argued. But Jesus told Peter that he needed to humble himself and be washed by his Master.

In those hours before he went to the cross, Jesus demonstrated to his disciples that if they were to be washed spiritually, he alone had the power. He alone was qualified. To be his disciples, they needed to humble themselves and acknowledge their need for Jesus' cleansing. Kneeling by Peter's dirty feet, Jesus explained, "If I do not wash you, you have no share with me" (John 13:8).

2. *Jesus was teaching the disciples to serve one another.* It is as though Jesus were explaining it this way: "Men, consider for a moment who I am. You call me 'Teacher' and 'Lord.' That's right. That's who I am. Now if I, with my position of power and authority have washed your feet, then you, my followers, should wash one another's feet" (from John 13, paraphrase mine).

Here is how the apostle John, in his Gospel, recounts what he heard that Passover evening: "I have given you an example, that you also should do just as I have done to you. Truly, truly, I say to you, a servant is not greater than his master, nor is a messenger greater than the one who sent him. If you know these things, blessed are you if you do them" (John 13:15–17).

It's as though Jesus said, "Quit debating who is the greatest. Instead, follow my example. Use your ability and authority not to promote yourselves, but to serve one another."

Less than a week earlier, Jesus had addressed this same issue, saying, "You know that the rulers of the Gentiles lord it over them, and their great ones exercise authority over them. It shall not be so among you. But whoever would be great among you must be your servant, and whoever would be first among you must be your slave, even as the Son of Man came not to be served but to serve, and to give his life as a ransom for many" (Matthew 20:25–28).

Walking Like Jesus in Servanthood

In that upper room, Jesus taught two essential truths to us as well:

1. *Jesus wants to serve us through spiritual cleansing.* Jesus demonstrated that if we have not yet humbled ourselves, acknowledging our need to be washed by Jesus, we cannot serve him. Again, Jesus said, "The Son of Man came not to be served but to serve, and to give his life as a ransom for many" (Matthew 20:28). He gave his life to buy us back from our sin.

Scripture says, "There are those who are clean in their own eyes but are not washed of their filth" (Proverbs 30:12). God demands that each of us allow the Savior to wash us clean from the filth of our sin. Following Jesus means abandoning all proud attempts to clean ourselves up and accepting what Jesus did for us through his sacrifice at Calvary. The blood of Jesus, the precious Lamb of God, washes us clean.

2. *Jesus wants us to serve others to bring him glory.* God has given each of us certain abilities and spheres of influence and authority. We can use that authority to promote ourselves or to serve others. But Jesus made his instruction clear when he said, "I have given you an example, that you also should do just as I have done to you" (John 13:15).

"Walking like Jesus" means reflecting his servant lifestyle—every day.

Here's a thought-provoking question: When those who know me best watch my life, do I remind them of Jesus?

- True servants of the Lord Jesus Christ don't push others out of the way on a quest for success. They help those on the rungs above and below them.

- True servants of Christ serve him wherever he calls them, whether they receive recognition or not.

- True servants of Christ keep serving him even if someone else gets credit for their work.

- True servants of Christ don't wait to be served. They take the initiative in serving others.

Our church was rocked at the unexpected news of Ed's death. Though in his early 70s, he looked fit and was very active. For more than a generation, Ed was a model of servanthood in our church. It didn't matter if Ed was on the official Sunday greeters' schedule or not, he was always there, actively looking for people to help as they made their way into our building.

It was typical for Ed to jog toward arriving young families in the parking lot to help carry a diaper bag or a young child—or both. And, if Ed were anywhere near the front door, no one needed to reach for the handle. Ed would hold it open, greeting friends old and new with his big smile and quiet voice.

Then, one Sunday, Ed wasn't there.

Before church, one family had discussed the death of "Mr. Ed," and as their car entered the parking lot, their young child asked her parents, "Who will open the door for us?"

I'm sure there were tears in the eyes of her parents when she proposed, "Maybe we can take Mr. Ed's place. Maybe we can open the door for others."

Yes, maybe we all can open doors for others—wherever the Lord has put us.

Ultimately, a good question to ask is this: Do my coworkers or classmates know me as someone who *uses* people or as someone who *serves* people?

Serving Christ can mean mirroring his character in less-than-glamorous ministries, such as fixing a meal for a sick person, driving a cancer patient to an oncology treatment, cleaning house for a bereaved church member, giving a financial gift anonymously, or holding the door open for others.

Diotrephes, in the New Testament, was known in his church as a man who loved to put himself first (3 John 9). How sad! Remember, Jesus came "not to be served, but to serve and give his life!" And God has given each of us abilities and resources to use for his glory in serving others in the church and in the community. How it would bring honor to our Father if we were all constantly looking for ways we could serve our brothers and sisters!

Often, the real tests of a servant's heart are at home. When we have a position of authority in the home as a husband, a mother, or an older sibling, we may expect, even demand, our family members to serve us or take care of our needs first. But how much sweeter, like our Lord, to use our position of authority to serve the others in our home!

God may call us to serve a disabled or homebound relative. He may show us a discouraged relative who needs encouragement through words and acts of kindness. Maybe we could put our interests aside and help a family member who is overloaded with current responsibilities. In Christ's love, we can "wash the feet" of a spouse, parents, grandparents, children, grandchildren, and siblings. What a great way to walk like Jesus!

Alas, and did my Saviour bleed?
And did my Sovereign die?
Would He devote that sacred head
For such a worm as I?

Was it for crimes that I have done,
He groaned upon the tree?
Amazing pity! grace unknown!
And love beyond degree!

Well might the sun in darkness hide,
And shut his glories in,

When Christ, the mighty Maker, died
For man, the creature's sin.

But drops of grief can ne'er repay
The debt of love I owe:
Here, Lord, I give myself away,
'Tis all that I can do!

—Isaac Watts

Discussion Questions

SERVING LIKE JESUS

1. Read aloud John 13:1–17. What do you think John's purpose was in prefacing his recounting of the footwashing incident with the comments in the first three verses? How can this "prologue" shape your own commitment to serve others?

2. Why do you think Peter at first resisted Jesus' attempt to wash his feet? In what ways do you relate to Peter?

3. How would you answer this question: Do my coworkers or fellow students know me as someone who uses people or someone who serves people? What changes do you believe the Lord wants to work in your life regarding serving others at work or school?

4. Whose feet do you believe the Lord would have you wash (figuratively speaking) in your church? Spend time asking the Lord to direct you to a fellow church member whom you might serve this week.

5. In your home, what are some ways you can reflect Jesus Christ by serving your family members?

6. Spend some time praying, "Lord, make me a Christlike servant." In your prayer, explore with the Lord your various relationships and life situations, asking him to use you in serving others.

7. If you are doing this study with a group, plan a literal footwashing during which you and your fellow group members wash one another's feet, mirroring Jesus' service to his disciples in the upper room.

Chapter 14
WALKING IN JOY LIKE JESUS

Did you ever notice that many of history's most famous artists (such as Leonardo da Vinci, Raphael, and Rembrandt) painted Jesus as somber—even sad and gloomy? That's understandable when we remember Isaiah's prophecy that the Messiah would be "a man of sorrows and acquainted with grief" (Isaiah 53:3). Even in our era, many people picture a somber Jesus when they think of him.

Yet, as Jesus prepared his heart for his soon-coming execution, he prayed that his followers would have within them "the full measure" of Jesus' joy (John 17:13 NIV).

Jesus, Our Model for Joy

The full measure of Jesus' joy? Imagine! A joyful Jesus! Where do we see a joyful Jesus in Scripture?

1. *We can see Jesus' joy in various situations.* Think about some of the scenarios recorded in the Gospels. For example, children were drawn to Jesus (Mark 10:13–16). Have you ever noticed the people to whom children gravitate? On whose lap do children feel free to climb? Children are not normally drawn to people who have a sad, sour demeanor but rather to warm, happy people—people of joy.

2. *We can see Jesus' joy in his actions.* We can also see Jesus' joy in his attendance at festive occasions, such as weddings and feasts. Jesus participated in the wedding of Cana. The newly converted Matthew threw a party—with Jesus the guest of honor.

For these and other events, Jesus drew slanderous criticism from some of the dour religious leaders. In his holy disappointment with these critics, Jesus asked rhetorically, "to what shall I compare this generation? It is like children sitting in the marketplaces and calling to their playmates, 'We played the flute for you, and you did not dance; we sang a dirge, and you did not mourn.' For John came neither eating nor drinking, and they say, 'He has a demon.' The Son of Man came eating and drinking, and they say, 'Look at him! A glutton and a drunkard, a friend of tax collectors and sinners!' Yet wisdom is justified by her deeds" (Matthew 11:16–19).

Jesus was pointing out the stark contrast between his lifestyle and the austere demeanor and Spartan lifestyle of John the Baptist. So what might we infer from those spiteful words from Jesus' enemies? In his book *The Character of Jesus,* Charles Edward Jefferson wrote, "They are the most precious bits of slander that ever slipped from slimy lips. They prove indisputably that whatever Jesus was or was not, he was not morose or sour or melancholy."[24]

It's true. When Jesus was present, joy was present! Jesus himself asked, "Can the wedding guests mourn as long as the bridegroom is with them?" (Matthew 9:15).

3. *We can see Jesus' joy in Scripture's explicit statements.* God's Word clearly says that Jesus was a man of joy. For example, when the seventy-two "missionaries" that Jesus sent out returned with their encouraging report, Jesus was "full of joy" (Luke 10:21 NIV).

Amazingly, the most explicit joyful comments from the lips of the Savior, recorded in God's Word, came only hours before his crucifixion. On that evening in the upper room with his closest followers, Jesus explained the importance of abiding in his love and obeying him. Then he said, "These things I have spoken to you, that my joy may be in you, and that your joy may be full" (John 15:11).

Then, as we saw earlier in this chapter, he prayed to his heavenly Father, "I am coming to you now, but I say these things while I am still in the world, so that they may have the full measure of my joy within them." (John 17:13 NIV).

What wonderful evidence to refute the idea of a gloomy Jesus! Jesus was a man of *joy.* But *why?* What was the source of this joy?

Certainty, Not Circumstances

Was Jesus joyful because he lived an easy life? Hardly. Jesus knew the normal difficulties of a first-century Palestinian craftsman. Life could be hard. Jesus probably had to labor long hours in his carpenter shop to help support his mother and younger half-siblings.

Add to those everyday challenges the pain of being misunderstood and eventually rejected by the great majority of his people. Jesus, the sinless One, no doubt felt sin's effects more sharply than we would. Our sensitivities are calloused by sin. So, we cannot explain Jesus' joy by thinking he lived a life marinated in pleasant circumstances.

Neither was Jesus joyful because he was somehow immune to pain and disappointment. New Testament professor Robert Law wrote, "No one has ever sounded the depths of reality, has ever penetrated to the ultimate core of life, as Jesus did."[25] Oh, the agony Jesus must have felt, not only from the nails that pierced him, but from the horror of being sinless yet becoming sin for us!

Although living as a "man of sorrows, and acquainted with grief," Jesus described himself as a man of joy even as he approached the horrors of his crucifixion. Where did he get such joy? The Bible often links joy to faith, hope, and love. Joy is often found in the context of certainty—of being sure. And Jesus was, indeed, *certain* of several things.

1. *Jesus was certain of his identity.* At Jesus' baptism we see the deep certainty of his loving relationship with his heavenly Father. Picture the thirty-year-old, dripping-wet Jesus standing on the bank of the Jordan River. Matthew's Gospel tells us that at the moment Jesus came out of the water, heaven opened. God's Spirit lighted on him, and a voice called down from heaven: "This is my beloved Son, with whom I am well pleased" (3:16–17).

How reassuring those words must have been to Jesus, even as God's Spirit led him from the Jordan River to his wilderness temptations. We can only wonder whether Jesus reflected on his Father's reassuring words during the struggles of the ensuing weeks and months.

Jesus heard his Father's declaration of love not only at the beginning of his public ministry, but also toward the end. On the Mount of Transfiguration, the Father once again spoke those comforting words, "This is my beloved Son, with whom I am well pleased; listen to him" (Matthew 17:5).

We saw this link between Jesus' joy and his certainty of his Father's love in the previous chapter on serving like Jesus. In the upper room on the night before the crucifixion, Jesus said to his disciples, "As the Father has loved me, so have I loved you. Abide in my love. If you keep my commandments, you will abide in my love, just as I have kept my Father's commandments and abide in his love. These things I have spoken to you, that my joy may be in you, and that your joy may be full" (John 15:9–11).

Did you catch that? Jesus spoke assuredly of the love the Father had for him and the love he had for his disciples. Then Jesus encouraged them to remember that the Father's love for him and his love for them could bring them joy.

The *certainty* of his identity as the much-loved Son of his Father brought Jesus *joy*—even as he contemplated being nailed to the cross in a matter of hours.

2. *Jesus was certain of his purpose.* John 15 also addresses another element of certainty that brings joy. Jesus said, "I have kept my Father's commandments" (John 15:10).

Our Lord repeatedly told others that he was not pursuing his own agenda but his Father's. For example, in John 6:38 we read this statement from Jesus: "I have come down from heaven, not to do my own will but the will of him who sent me." Jesus was certain not only of his identity as God's Son but also of his calling. He had a certainty of *purpose*. He knew the joy of serving his heavenly Father.

Shortly before his arrest, Jesus prayed, "I glorified you on earth, having accomplished the work that you gave me to do" (John 17:4). Serving *self* brings only a shallow, temporary happiness but, as Jesus knew, doing the will of our heavenly Father brings real joy.

3. *Jesus was certain of his goal.* Jesus knew where he was going. He had a confident, forward look. His heavenly Father had placed a goal before him, and pursuing that goal brought Jesus joy. He saw his

earthly life and ministry from an *eternal* perspective. He saw beyond the weariness, rejection, and pain of this life to the eternal destiny laid out for him. Remember, the writer of Hebrews urged us to be "looking to Jesus, the founder and perfecter of our faith, who for the *joy* that was set before him endured the cross, despising the shame, and is seated at the right hand of the throne of God" (Hebrews 12:2, emphasis added).

Jesus was certain of this goal. He had come to this sin-infected, pain-filled earth to redeem the people his heavenly Father had given him. Even though accomplishing that goal meant enduring the pain and shame of the cross, Jesus pursued that goal with joy.

In *Glimpses of the Inner Life of Christ,* William Blaikie wrote, "Such a vision of the future, rising out of darkness and confusion of the present, would send a gleam of heaven into the heart of Jesus, and kindle in His countenance a radiance of holy joy."[26] Think of that! Jesus was indeed characterized by joy despite the pain he felt more sharply than we do. Often our sin dulls our emotions. We begin to grow calluses on our hearts as we attempt to protect ourselves from the pain of being sinned against–again. But Jesus fully felt all the pain.

The Bible links Jesus' joy with the certainty—the confidence— he had in his *identity* as the much-loved Son of God, his *purpose* of doing the will of his Father, and his *goal* of arriving in heaven, having accomplished his mission of redeeming his people.

Walking in Joy Like Jesus

How it must delight the heart of our heavenly Father when his children live joyfully! Unfortunately, some dour Christians give the impression that the more somber the person, the more spiritual he or she must be.

However, twentieth-century philosopher Elton Trueblood wrote in his book *The Humor of Christ,* "Any alleged Christianity which fails to express itself in cheerfulness, at some point, is clearly spurious."[27] That is a bold statement. Was he right?

The Christians described in the New Testament reflected Jesus' joy. For example, the church in Jerusalem was marked by these characteristics: "Attending the temple together and breaking bread in their homes, they received their food with glad and generous hearts" (Acts 2:46). The picture is one of remarkable joy.

Even though the early Christians in Pisidia were persecuted by nonbelievers, the author of the book of Acts remarked, "The disciples were filled with joy and with the Holy Spirit" (Acts 13:52).

The New Testament also contains repeated *commands* to be joyful:

- "Rejoice in hope" (Romans 12:12).
- "Rejoice in the Lord" (Philippians 3:1).
- "Rejoice in the Lord always; again I will say, rejoice" (Philippians 4:4).
- "Rejoice always" (1 Thessalonians 5:16).

Paul explained that joy is a byproduct of a close relationship to Christ, being controlled by the Holy Spirit, and belonging to God's kingdom.

- To the Galatian believers he wrote that "the fruit of the Spirit is... joy" (5:22).
- To the Roman believers he pointed out that the very "kingdom of God is ... righteousness and peace and joy in the Holy Spirit" (14:17).

The New Testament abounds with portrayals of joyful Christians. And throughout history, followers of Christ have been known for their joy. I believe Trueblood's assertion is correct that Christianity without joy is spurious, fake, phony.

The Source of Our Joy: Certainty, Not Circumstances

So, what is the source of the Christian's joy? We can't depend on our circumstances to bring us joy. God hasn't promised us lives free from pain and frustration. We all endure trials and troubles. And God hasn't given us some divine miracle drug to dull the pain of living in a heartbreaking, violent, evil world. No, we may mourn even more deeply than our non-Christian neighbors because we are so aware of the painful effects of sin in our lives and in the world around us (Matthew 5:4).

What is the basis of the Christian's joy, then? Our joy is like our Master's joy. This joy comes from a foundational *certainty*—a sureness.

1. *We can find our joy in the certainty of our identity.* Like Christ's joy, our joy depends less on what we have or what is happening to us than on who we are or, specifically, Whose we are. The knowledge that God calls us his chosen children brings the Christian true joy. "See what kind of love the Father has given to us, that we should be called children of God; and so we are" (1 John 3:1). As his children, we can also claim this identity: *citizens of heaven.* Jesus said, "Rejoice that your names are written in heaven" (Luke 10:20). Believers can find great joy in remembering the change God has worked in us: guilty, condemned sinners now forgiven, adopted children of God.

We see this kind of joy in new believers in Scripture too. The forgiven, newly baptized Ethiopian "went on his way rejoicing" (Acts 8:39). And the Philippian jailer "rejoiced along with his entire household that he had believed in God" (Acts 16:34).

God replaced enslavement to sin with freedom in Christ. He turned condemnation into salvation. The Father's frown transformed into a smile. British theologian Octavius Winslow wrote, "The religion of Christ is the religion of joy. Christ came to take away our sins, to roll off our curse, to unbind our chains, to open our prison house, to cancel our debt; in a word, to give us the oil of joy for mourning, the garment of praise for the spirit of heaviness."[28]

We have a new relationship with God because of what Christ did on our behalf. Paul wrote, "Since we have been justified by faith, we have peace with God through our Lord Jesus Christ. Through him we have also obtained access by faith into this grace in which we stand, and we rejoice in hope of the glory of God" (Romans 5:1–2).

2. *We can find our joy in the certainty of our purpose.* We are servants of the Most High God! And doing what pleases him floods us with joy. By contrast, pursuing our own pleasure and happiness eventually yields only dryness and disappointment. Imagine the joy in every

faithful Christian's heart who hears on that great day, "Well done, good and faithful servant. You have been faithful over a little; I will set you over much. Enter into the joy of your master" (Matthew 25:21).

3. *We can find our joy in the certainty of our goal.* Like our Lord, we Christians know the joy of *certainty* in where we are headed—the certainty of God's goal for us. Our lives are not meaningless. Everything God has providentially brought into our lives is moving us toward his ultimate objective for us. We can even face painful times with a profound sense of joy.

Paul, who knew personal suffering well, wrote, "We rejoice in our sufferings, knowing that suffering produces endurance, and endurance produces character, and character produces hope" (Romans 5:3–4).

James echoed Paul's teaching: "Count it all joy, my brothers, when you meet trials of various kinds, for you know that the testing of your faith produces steadfastness" (James 1:2–3). Realizing that suffering is purposeful, moving us toward God's goal for us, enables us to have true joy. We can view our temporal difficulties in light of eternity. The words of the Holy Spirit through Peter, in 1 Peter 1:6–9, bring assurance to our souls during times of suffering:

> In this you rejoice, though now for a little while, if necessary, you have been grieved by various trials, so that the tested genuineness of your faith—more precious than gold that perishes though it is tested by fire—may be found to result in praise and glory and honor at the revelation of Jesus Christ. Though you have not seen him, you love him. Though you do not now see him, you believe in him and rejoice with joy that is inexpressible and filled with glory, obtaining the outcome of your faith, the salvation of your souls.

4. *We find our ultimate joy in Christ himself.* Even greater than the joy that comes from knowing our identity, our purpose, and our goal, is the joy we find in our ultimate foundation. We have Jesus Christ himself as our Chief Joy. He is the fountainhead from which flows

all other joys. On the night before Jesus was taken away from his disciples for the three days of his arrest, trial, crucifixion, and burial, he assured them that their grief would turn to joy. And what would be the motivating force behind their restored joy?

Jesus said, "You have sorrow now, but I will see you again, and your hearts will rejoice, and no one will take your joy from you" (John 16:22). The promised presence of Jesus Christ himself is the Christian's ultimate joy!

> Jesus, I am resting, resting
> In the joy of what Thou art;
> I am finding out the greatness
> Of Thy loving heart.
> Thou hast bid me gaze upon thee,
> And Thy beauty fills my soul,
> For by Thy transforming power,
> Thou hast made me whole."

—Jean Sophia Pigott

Discussion Questions

WALKING IN JOY LIKE JESUS

1. Share with the people in your group a story from the Gospels that depicts Jesus as joyful. Or read it again for yourself if you're doing this study alone. Why are you drawn to this story?

2. Why was Jesus joyful? What were the sources of his joy?

3. What is the source of the Christian's joy?

4. Why do Christians sometimes lack joy?

5. If you feel comfortable doing so, share the story of a time when you lost your sense of joy. As you reflect on that time, what is it that you may have lost sight of? What has helped (or could help) you regain the joy of the Lord?

6. Read Psalm 51:12 in context. Then spend time making the prayer of this verse your personal request to the Lord.

Chapter 15
LOVING LIKE JESUS

HAVE YOU EVER WONDERED WHAT WAS THE GREATEST ACT OF LOVE—EVER? We can read the *Guinness World Records* book and find the ultimate example of almost anything: the greatest altitude ever achieved by man or woman, the greatest depth a human being has ever descended into the ocean, the greatest speed ever attained by any individual, and so on. What if Guinness had a category for the greatest act of love? What entry would we find there?

No doubt some would say, "There's no way anyone could ever decide that." However, one particular act of love in all of history is the quintessence of love. It makes all others pale in comparison.

One specific example has been documented as the supreme act of love in the whole history of humanity: Jesus himself foreshadowed his sacrifice on the cross when he said, "Greater love has no one than this, that someone lay down his life for his friends" (John 15:13).

Jesus' Supreme Love

The apostle John wrote, "This is how we know what love is: Jesus Christ laid down his life for us" (1 John 3:16 NIV). The Bible is crystal clear. The all-time act of love transcending all others is Jesus' death on the cross in the place of undeserving sinners—you and me. What makes Jesus' crucifixion the ultimate expression of love? What are some of his love's qualities?

1. *Jesus' love was purely voluntary.* He was not a helpless victim of the Jewish leaders who manipulated his execution, nor of the Roman soldiers who carried out his crucifixion. No one made Jesus go to the cross. He willingly died in our place. Jesus himself explained, "I lay

down my life for the sheep…. No one takes it from me, but I lay it down of my own accord. I have authority to lay it down and authority to take it up again" (John 10:15, 18).

Jesus chose to die for us because he loved us.

2. *Jesus' love was substitutionary.* You and I have to die. When our forefather Adam chose to sin against God, death entered the human race (Genesis 2:17). Every sinful human born since then has been "destined to die" (Hebrews 9:27 NIV). We know that unless the Lord returns first, we will all die. Our deaths are the inevitable result of the "sin genes" inherited from our father Adam. And we see the evidence in our own many, many sins.

However, Jesus did not have to die. As God incarnate, Jesus was the very "Author of life" (Acts 3:15). He was the Eternal One walking here on earth as a human being. Jesus was different from all other human beings in this significant way: He had no sin. (See 2 Corinthians 5:21; Hebrew 4:15; 1 Peter 2:22; 1 John 3:5.) Because he had no sin, Jesus did not have to die.

So, if Jesus didn't have to die, why did he? Remember, Jesus said, "I lay down my life for the sheep" (John 10:15). That little preposition *for* is so significant. It means "in the place of." Peter later echoed the Savior's explanation for his death when he wrote, "Christ also suffered once for sins, the righteous for [same word as in John 10:15] the unrighteous, that he might bring us to God" (1 Peter 3:18, brackets added). We sinners deserve to die for our sins, but the sinless Jesus took our place on that Roman cross. He died instead of us. He died the death you and I should have died. Jesus died in our place as an expression of his amazing love.

3. *Jesus' love was sacrificial.* Jesus' love for us was more than "talk." He put his love into action in the most astonishing way. He sacrificially gave his precious, perfect life for us.

Jesus' words bear repeating: "Greater love has no one than this, that someone lay down his life for his friends" (John 15:13).

Many Christians struggle during painful circumstances or seasons of depression. I remember one young man who came to see me. Not long after he had committed his life to Christ, his wife packed her bags and announced, "I don't want you, and I don't want your

God." He was stunned. He found himself alone, left to raise their toddler son by himself.

I can still see him, his head bowed in discouragement, his voice quavering. "Pastor, does God really love me?" he asked.

There was no denying his profound pain. I could not promise that his life would be sunnier tomorrow. What could I say? Through my own tears, I pointed him to the cross of his newfound Savior. Though this man's world was shaken, the love of Christ remained sure. The cross stood as an unmoving monument of God's love for this hurting young man.

Jesus laid down his life for us, paying the ultimate price, despite the fact that we are so undeserving. Paul wrote, "While we were still weak, at the right time Christ died for the ungodly. For one will scarcely die for a righteous person—though perhaps for a good person one would dare even to die— but God shows his love for us in that while we were still sinners, Christ died for us" (Romans 5:6–8).

4. *Jesus' love was personal.* Just think of how *personal* the love of our Savior is! Sometimes we focus so much on the truth that "God so loved the world" (John 3:16), that we don't fully grasp the intensely personal love Jesus has for each one of us. Who was on Jesus' mind and heart as he prepared to lay down his life on the cross? Jesus himself tells us. In those anguished hours before the cross, he let his followers eavesdrop as he interceded for all those who follow him: "I am praying for them. I am not praying for the world but for those whom you have given me" (John 17:9).

Every believer in Jesus Christ can say with astonished gratitude, "I was on his heart even as he laid down his life on the cross." We each can repeat the words of Paul, "The life I now live in the flesh I live by faith in the Son of God, who loved me and gave himself for me" (Galatians 2:20).

John Piper wrote, "Surely this is the way we should understand the sufferings and death of Christ. They have to do with me. They are about Christ's love for me personally. It is *my* sin that cuts me off from God, not sin in general. It is *my* hard-heartedness and spiritual numbness that demean the worth of Christ." Piper continues several paragraphs later, "My heart is swayed, and I embrace the beauty and bounty of Christ my treasure. And there flows into my heart this great reality—the love of Christ for me. So I say with those early witnesses, "He loved me and gave himself for me."[29]

How soul-gripping it is to realize how immensely he loves you and me—personally!

We revel in the realization that nothing "will be able to separate us from the love of God in Christ Jesus our Lord" (Romans 8:39). The undeserved love—the ill-deserved love—Jesus has for us as his followers is more than something to be enjoyed. God expects us to replicate it in our own lives. When we truly grasp Jesus' love for us, it has a demonstrable effect on how we treat one another in the body of Christ.

Walking Like Jesus in Love for One Another

God calls us, as Christians, to be like our Savior. This is not merely a suggestion. It is an obligation. As we have noted from the outset, "By this we may know that we are in him: whoever says he abides in him ought to walk in the same way in which he walked" (1 John 2:5–6).

Mirroring Jesus' character specifically applies to our relationship with other believers. In John's Gospel, he recalls Jesus' words: "A new commandment I give to you, that you love one another: just as I have loved you, you also are to love one another" (John 13:34).

Decades later, as an older man, John told his readers, "By this we know love, that he laid down his life for us, and we ought to lay down our lives for the brothers" (1 John 3:16).

What does this love look like in practical terms?

1. *God calls us to a voluntary love.* Choosing to love certain people can be so difficult at times. But, as we saw above, Christ said we "must love one another." Our Savior has both commanded and modeled this love. Walking like Jesus in love means submitting to our sovereign Savior, obeying his commands daily.

Love is a sacrificial giving of oneself for the welfare of someone else—even if that other person is unresponsive or undeserving.

Ebony demonstrated that kind of love. The staff in the memory care unit of the local nursing home appreciated Ebony so much—

even though they were a bit baffled by her. Every week on her day off from the hair salon, she would come for a few hours to "prettify" (as she called it) some of the residents. Most of the ladies she served had lost their capacity to show Ebony any meaningful appreciation. So, what motivated her to love the unresponsive? She walked in love as Jesus did.

What can motivate *us* to love the unappreciative, the unlovely, and even the unlovable? This is a common struggle.

New Testament scholar, D. A. Carson admitted, "The unlovely ones in the brotherhood bring out the worst in me. The whiners get on my nerves. The gossips and the arrogant, the immature and the silly, conspire to drain my resolve."[30] So, what hope is there that any of us could love those difficult-to-love brothers and sisters in Christ—or even members of our own families?

Frequently our attitude is something like this: I'll love you as long as I like you. Or I'll love you as I feel loved by you. We could call this "reactionary love." Here's another way we could put it: As long as I feel sufficiently loved by you, I will do my best to love you back, but if I don't feel loved enough by you, then I cannot and will not love you.

But if we rely on other people—spouse, parents, children, brothers and sisters in Christ—to "fill our love tanks" in order to have enough love to give back, we will quickly find ourselves running on empty.

There is a much more reliable source for sufficiently filled "love tanks." The apostle John explains it this way in 1 John 4:

- "Beloved, let us love one another, for love is from God" (v. 7).

- "Beloved, if God so loved us, we also ought to love one another" (v. 11).

- "We know and rely on the love God has for us" (v. 16 NIV).

- "We love because he first loved us" (v. 19).

We could call this "overflowing love."

In other words, instead of depending on other people to supply our outflowing love, our Lord calls us to rely on the love we have already received from him.

We can draw upon Christ's infinite, never-ending love. After all, without him, we can do nothing (John 15:5). Through him, we can do all things (Philippians 4:13). Knowing and relying on the love the Lord has for us, we can, in turn, choose (a voluntary act) to love even the most unlovable person.

2. *God calls us to a substitutionary love.* We followers of Christ can mirror Jesus' love for us by loving one another in a *substitutionary* way. Walking in love like Jesus means that when we see our brothers and sisters in need, we involve ourselves in their lives. Paul stated it this way: "Bear one another's burdens, and so fulfill the law of Christ" (Galatians 6:2). The heart of the "law of Christ" is his command: "Love one another as I have loved you" (John 15:12).

To demonstrate the love of Christ is to come alongside our brothers and sisters, sharing their emotional and spiritual struggles, lightening their load. Substitutionary love supports and encourages others because of Christ's love for us.

3. *God calls us to sacrificial love.* Jesus did more than declare his love for us in words. He also demonstrated his love for us in action—*sacrificial* action. True followers of Jesus Christ do their best to emulate that kind of Christlike, sacrificial love.

That love becomes very practical. John (often called the apostle of love) taught, "By this we know love, that he laid down his life for us, and we ought to lay down our lives for the brothers. But if anyone has the world's goods and sees his brother in need, yet closes his heart against him, how does God's love abide in him? Little children, let us not love in word or talk but in deed and in truth" (1 John 3:16–18).

If we want to love others as Christ has loved us, we cannot lock the doors of our hearts against those in need. A closed-hearted Christian is an oxymoron—a contradiction in terms! God commands us to love our brothers and sisters in tangible, sacrificial ways. When we become aware of others' needs, he tells us to willingly share the resources he has entrusted to us. If we have any money, any clothes, any vehicles, any food—whatever—God expects us to share willingly what we have with those in need.

Our Lord sacrificed his life for us. How amazingly loving! How can recipients of our Lord's generous love be stingy when we see our brothers and sisters in material, emotional, or spiritual need? Every day, remember the words of our Lord: "Love one another as I have loved you" (John 15:12).

4. *God calls us to a personal love.* Sometimes we are willing to love others as long as we don't have to get too close. Putting money in the offering plate or sending money to a Christian relief agency salves the conscience. Yet Paul pricks our conscience: "Let love be genuine.... Love one another with brotherly affection.... Contribute to the needs of the saints and seek to show hospitality.... Rejoice with those who rejoice, weep with those who weep" (Romans 12:9–10, 13, 15).

Our Lord loved people in a very personal way. He cared about every individual. Recall how he demonstrated love to Matthew the tax collector, the woman at the well, the leper, the demon-possessed man, Saul of Tarsus—even you and me.

As we seek to love as he loved, he wants us to mirror his love personally.

Loving like Jesus may mean spending time one-on-one with a person struggling with an addiction. Loving like Jesus may mean encouraging a parent who has a rebellious child. Loving like Jesus may mean helping someone unemployed to create a strong résumé. Loving like Jesus may mean simply sitting for a while with a brother or sister with a chronic disease.

Personal, Christlike love reaches out to others—even if it moves us out of our comfort zones. Brian and Andrea weren't looking for more to do, but they felt the Holy Spirit prompting them to reach out to Tiffany after a providential meeting at the supermarket.[31] Andrea and Tiffany hadn't visited since the two ladies graduated from high school together.

Within a few minutes Brian and Andrea realized that Tiffany's life was in chaos. Her live-in boyfriend was doing drugs, and Tiffany feared for her young daughter's safety. Andrea invited Tiffany to come for coffee the next morning after the kids left for school. So began a journey over the following months—a journey of Brian and Andrea showing Tiffany the love of Christ. They talked with her, prayed with her, shared the good news of Christ with her, and even let Tiffany and her daughter stay with them for a few days when Tiffany's boyfriend was at his worst.

Over time, the Lord used Brian and Andrea's love to melt Tiffany's heart and bring her to faith in Jesus. At Tiffany's baptism later that year, Brian and Andrea publicly gave thanks for God's kindness in giving them a love for Tiffany that moved them out of their comfort zone.

Jesus is our ultimate example of practical love. What joy we can find if we commit to loving as he loves!

> See, from His head, His hands, His feet,
> Sorrow and love flow mingled down;
> Did e'er such love and sorrow meet,
> Or thorns compose so rich a crown?
> Were the whole realm of nature mine,
> That were a present far too small;
> Love so amazing, so divine,
> Demands my soul, my life, my all.

> —Isaac Watts

Discussion Questions
LOVING LIKE JESUS

1. In your own words, retell a story from the Bible that highlights one way Jesus demonstrated love. What draws you to this story?

2. What qualities of Jesus' love do you see in his death on the cross?

3. As described in this chapter, what is reactionary love? Why is this type of love so unreliable?

4. How does this chapter describe overflowing love? Describe this concept in your own words. Read through 1 John 4:7–21 before formulating your answer.

5. Think of a person you find especially difficult to love. Talk to God about your struggle. Ask him to give you opportunities this week to mirror Christ's love to that person.

Chapter 16

THE COST OF WALKING LIKE JESUS

SPAM. WE ALL GET THOSE UNSOLICITED EMAILS IN OUR INBOX. HOW long would you linger over an ad for a product that looks suspicious yet strangely inviting?

"You can get this fabulous ring—with 'real diamonades' and overlaid with genuine 14-karat gold—for only $19.99! And, if you order *now*, we will also send you this matching set of earrings!"

Have you already ordered *your* genuine diamonade ring? Why not? What's holding you back? Is it because you smell a fake? Who wants a cheap imitation?

Cheap imitations don't cost much. But they're not worth much either.

Tragically, many professing Christians today are like those diamonade rings with an overlay of genuine gold. They look nice. They appear genuine Christians, yet they are nothing more than cheap imitations.

What if each of us took a hard look at our daily lives—our passions and priorities? How differently are we living than the non-Christians around us? Are we pursuing the same things as our unbelieving coworkers and neighbors—only with an "overlay" of Christianity?

Let me encourage you to humbly ask yourself, "Am I a genuine Christian or merely a cheap imitation?" That's what the apostle Paul urges us, too: "Examine yourselves, to see whether you are in the faith. Test yourselves" (2 Corinthians 13:5).

Sometimes we're not sure. In his younger years, John Wesley (the founder of Methodism) seemed to have much going for him in the realm of religion. He grew up in a highly devout home, trained in theology at Oxford, and was ordained in the Anglican Church. Those who knew him well would testify that he was highly disciplined, devoting hours to religious exercises and always trying to do the right thing.

But inwardly, Wesley was continually frustrated by his own repeated failures. One day a Moravian missionary asked Wesley if he had faith in Jesus Christ. He replied that he did, but later he reflected, "I fear they were vain words."

Some months later, John Wesley, an ordained pastor, highly regarded in religious circles, came to realize that his religion was merely external. Wesley had been professing to be a Christian, but his was merely a Christian "overlay." By God's amazing grace, Wesley later converted to saving faith and spent his remaining years as a true follower of Jesus Christ.

It's sobering, isn't it? How can we tell if we might be living with a mere Christian overlay? What does a genuine Christian look like, anyway?

At the beginning of our quest in this book, we said we need to change one crucial word. It's not *what* does a genuine Christian look like, but *Who* does a genuine Christian look like?

The apostle John put it this way: "By this we may know that we are in him: whoever says he abides in him ought to walk in the same way in which he walked" (1 John 2:5–6). Those who truly are in Christ will bear fruit—increasingly reflecting Christ. If someone is not living a Christlike life, his claim of being a Christian is suspicious. Genuine Christians do more than claim to belong to Christ. Their conduct backs up their verbal claim.

The Call and the Cost

Jesus stands before us, even as he stood before that Galilean crowd, and calls out, "Come to me, all who labor and are heavy laden, and I will give you rest. Take my yoke upon you, and learn from me, for I am gentle and lowly in heart, and you will find rest for your souls" (Matthew 11:28–29). Our gracious King commands us to step out of the crowd and learn from him. As we come to Jesus in faith, what do we see? We see his meekness, servanthood, compassion, joy, holiness, and more.

He gives us new life, and we begin to display these same Christ-reflecting traits. But answering Jesus' call has a cost.

I had just stepped off the platform after preaching an evangelistic message when a young man whom I had never seen before met me at the bottom step. Without any introduction, without any segue, he asked, "How much will it cost me to become a Christian?"

How would you answer that eternity-defining question?

I sat down with that young man and explained one of the great paradoxes of the gospel—the cost of becoming a Christ follower.

On one hand, following Jesus costs us nothing. Paul wrote, "The free gift of God is eternal life in Christ Jesus our Lord" (Romans 6:23). Becoming a Christian doesn't cost us anything. There's nothing we can pay to acquire eternal life. It is purely God's free gift.

On the other hand, following Jesus will cost us everything. Jesus himself laid out the cost of total commitment for people who contemplated following him: "If anyone comes to me and does not hate his own father and mother and wife and children and brothers and sisters, yes, and even his own life, he cannot be my disciple. Whoever does not bear his own cross and come after me cannot be my disciple" (Luke 14:26–27). After illustrating the urgency, Jesus said, "Any one of you who does not renounce all that he has cannot be my disciple" (Luke 14:33).

So, if we want to follow Jesus, he calls us to count the cost. A Christlike life will cost us everything. Jesus unapologetically declared, "If anyone would come after me, let him deny himself and take up his cross daily and follow me (Luke 9:23). What did he mean by that?

1. *The cost of self-denial.* First, Jesus said that if we are going to follow him, we must *deny* ourselves. He did not mean denying things *to* ourselves, the way some people give up candy or smoking for Lent. He is demanding that we give up *ourselves*! No more living for *self*-promotion, *self*-defense, *self*-esteem, or *self*-fulfillment. No more demanding our rights and our own ways. No more pursuing our own ambitions.

135

Jesus calls us to renounce our *selves*—to turn our backs on self and selfishness—and live totally committed to him.

2. *The cost of death to self.* Jesus commands us to "take up our cross daily." This cross doesn't symbolize a mere inconvenience. Some people call their arthritis, difficult boss, or lazy husband their cross to bear. But that's not what Jesus means. He uses the word *cross* here to symbolize not only suffering but *death*.

Committing ourselves to walking like Jesus requires taking up our symbol of death every day: Death to old desires and lifestyles. Death to our very *selves*. This is Paul's testimony in Galatians 2:20: "I have been crucified with Christ. It is no longer I who live, but Christ who lives in me."

3. *The cost of daily following.* To *follow* Christ means exactly what we've been exploring in this book—walking as Jesus did. God calls us to go *his* way, not deviating from the path he has "set before us" (Hebrews 12:1). That means not going to the right or the left but continuing in the footprints of the One who loved us so much he died for us!

Although a basic description of a Christian is a follower of Jesus Christ, many professing Christians, especially in western Christianity, follow a far different path from the one Jesus walked.

I shudder to think of the many imitation Christians who will hear those horrifying words from the lips of King Jesus on judgment day: "I never knew you; depart from me, you workers of lawlessness" (Matthew 7:23). Oh, Lord, do your work of grace in hearts of everyone who reads this book, that they might affirm their relationship with you today!

The Commitment

Following Jesus—walking in his steps—will cost us everything. Will you pay the price? Will you make that commitment? Listen to King Jesus and weigh his words carefully: "Whoever would save his life will lose it, but whoever loses his life for my sake and the gospel's will save it. For what does it profit a man to gain the whole world and forfeit his soul?" (Mark 8:35–36).

This is a warning from Jesus himself. If we decide that denying ourselves is too costly, that choice will condemn us eternally. By choosing to hang onto our *selves*—*self*-promotion, *self*-protection, *self*-assertion, *self*-happiness—we are choosing to forfeit our own souls.

Jesus knows those who are his. He cannot be fooled by our unsubstantiated *claims*. He sees right through the cheap overlay. Our lifestyles deny him. And on that most-important day, he will deny us. What an eternally foolish choice it is to hang onto what the world offers and forfeit our souls!

Please don't take that path! The world's ways may seem right. They may promise a more exciting life. But they end in death (Proverbs 14:12). According to our Lord, they actually end in hell (Luke 13:23–28).

Choose the right path. Take to heart the great promise of our Lord. If, in faith, we follow him alone, we will gladly turn our backs on the cheap imitation and lose our lives for him. And in losing our lives, we will truly find them. Our gracious Lord will give us his life, which will reflect his character. Abandoning our *selves* makes room for him to give us new life and energize us to follow him. Then we can live Christ-empowered, Christlike lives now and enjoy his glorious eternal life in heaven.

I never again saw the young man who asked, "How much will it cost me to become a Christian?" But I pray the Holy Spirit used our conversation to awaken him to his need for Christ and that one day I will see him in heaven.

The Best Offer Ever

Jesus offers us life that's the real thing—not a cheap knockoff. He paid a tremendous price to give us this gift. And he desperately wants followers who are genuine.

Remember, "By this we may know that we are in him: whoever says he abides in him ought to walk in the same way in which he walked" (1 John 2:5–6).

If we follow him alone, we will truly walk as Jesus walked.

137

More like the Master I would ever be,
More of His meekness, more humility;
More zeal to labor, more courage to be true,
More consecration for work He bids me do.
Take Thou my heart,
I would be Thine alone;
Take Thou my heart,
and make it all Thine own.
Purge me from sin,
O Lord, I now implore,
Wash me and keep me
Thine forevermore.

—Charles H. Gabriel

Discussion Questions

THE COST OF WALKING LIKE JESUS

1. According to 1 John 2:5–6, what is a key identifying mark of a true Christian?

2. In your own words, explain the phrase, "Take up your cross daily." What does it cost to follow Jesus Christ?

3. Without becoming spiritually abusive, how can our churches be more faithful in warning people of the danger of being mere imitation Christians?

4. Has the Holy Spirit convicted you that you have been living a lie? Are you realizing that you are not yet a true follower of Jesus Christ but a mere imitation with a little overlay of Jesus? Read Matthew 11:28–29. Will you obey the gracious command of King Jesus and ask him to forgive your sins and make you his child?

5. Has the Holy Spirit prompted you to make some changes in your commitment to follow Christ? Name a few. Take the words of Charles H. Gabriel's poem (found at the end of this chapter) and make them your personal prayer to God.

6. Commit to memorizing 1 John 2:5–6. Repeat this verse aloud to your study group or to an accountability partner the next time you meet.

Chapter 17

THE PRIVILEGE OF WALKING LIKE JESUS

"WHAT DO YOU WANT TO BE WHEN YOU GROW UP?" I ASKED A LITTLE BOY.

He looked at me and said with great enthusiasm, "When I grow up, I want to be a *man!*"

Not a bad goal for a little boy, is it?

Regardless of our age, we each could ask ourselves, "What do I want to be when I grow up?" More precisely, "What do I want to be when I grow up *spiritually?*"

If we attempt to paint a picture of spiritual maturity in *what* terms—what spiritual maturity looks like—our tendency will be to make a list. However, various individuals, churches, and denominations, come up with different items on their list.

Rather than trying to list what Christian maturity looks like, wouldn't it be better to ask, "*Who* does spiritual maturity look like?" The answer to that crucially important question is this: Spiritual maturity looks like Jesus! The desire of every growing Christian is to be more and more like Jesus—to more clearly reflect him in daily life.

English theologian John Stott wrote these heart-stirring words: "We want to be like Christ, and that thoroughly, profoundly, entirely. Nothing less than this will do."[32]

If Christlikeness is our heart's desire–our lifelong quest—how does that happen? What is the process? How can we grow to be more and more like Jesus every day?

The Bible answers that important question in 2 Corinthians 3:18: "We all, with unveiled face, beholding the glory of the Lord, are being transformed into the same image from one degree of glory to another. For this comes from the Lord who is the Spirit."

We can find two key words in this verse: *transformed* and *beholding*.

Transformed

In our most honest moments, we believers freely acknowledge our need for change, for transformation. We all still have sin in our lives, and some of those sins persistently cling to us. We recognize aspects of our spiritual immaturity. We want to change.

Sometimes people say, "I just want to be myself." They set goals to be a better person. But God calls you and me as followers of Jesus Christ, to a greater purpose than merely being ourselves. God wants so much more for us. And true followers of Jesus Christ set their hearts on this higher purpose: to be like Jesus, to reflect his character, and to "walk as Jesus." The good news is that his Spirit is actively, purposefully, involved in that transformation to "be conformed to the image of his Son" (Romans 8:29).

1. *Transformation's goal.* The goal of Christian maturity is Christlikeness. Jesus Christ is the model of what we are to become.

As we have seen before, the first Adam rebelled against the Creator and brought sin and its damaging effects on the whole human race. As our representative, the first Adam, muddled God's design for his image bearers. God had created human beings to reflect his glory in ways nothing else in creation could. However, because of Adam's sin, the human race failed to fulfill its purpose of perfectly reflecting God's glory.

Then Jesus came.

He came to this earth as a real human being, perfectly reflecting the Father's glory. The writer of Hebrews wrote that God's Son "is the radiance of the glory of God and the exact imprint of his nature" (1:3). Jesus, the perfect, sinless man, serves as the prototype of what God will do with all his redeemed people. Just as the "first man," Adam, brought sin and death to the human race, the "second man," Jesus Christ, brought redemption and life.

The apostle Paul explained God's goal for us as his image bearers this way: "Just as we have borne the likeness of the earthly man, so shall we bear the likeness of the man from heaven" (1 Corinthians 15:47–49).

We can't fully understand this now. But when Jesus returns to this earth, that transformation will be completed. The apostle John wrote, "Beloved, we are God's children now, and what we will be has not yet appeared; but we know that when he appears we shall be like him, because we shall see him as he is" (1 John 3:2).

From that glorious moment of ultimate transformation, we redeemed image bearers will finally fulfill our mission, perfectly reflecting God's glory by ruling over the new heavens and new earth as God's representatives. (See Revelation 22:5.) We anxiously await "graduation day," when God accomplishes that final transformation in us.

2. The Holy Spirit's role in transformation. Meanwhile, what is God doing in our lives? The apostle Paul says this change is already in process. We "are being transformed into the same image" (2 Corinthians 3:18). This transformation is not the result of some self-improvement plan. The change does not come through mere effort. It is the work of the Holy Spirit, producing the fruit of the Spirit in the lives of believers.

Those who are not yet believers in Christ cannot understand spiritual things. In 2 Corinthians the apostle Paul says that Satan has "blinded the minds of the unbelievers, to keep them from seeing the light of the gospel of the glory of Christ" (4:4).

Paul uses the analogy of a veil covering an unbeliever's heart. (See 2 Corinthians 3:15.) The good news is that "when one turns to the Lord, the veil is removed" (v. 16). Only Christ can take that veil away. The Holy Spirit draws us to Christ and takes the veil off our minds and hearts, so we can see Christ as Savior and Lord.

In a hymn called "Let Us Love and Sing and Wonder," John Newton wrote that the Holy Spirit "gave us ears and gave us eyes." No longer are we spiritually blind and insensitive to Christ. The Holy Spirit reveals Christ to us—not just at our conversion but daily. Part of the Holy Spirit's ministry is to reveal Christ and promote Christ to us. (See John 16:14.) As he continues to reveal Jesus Christ to us, we are changed—transformed.

3. *Transformation's gradual process.* What does that transformation process look like? It is not instantaneous but gradual and sure. In fact, our English word *metamorphosis* comes from the Greek word translated *transformed* in this verse. Metamorphosis implies a gradual-but-sure change from one form to another.

When I was a boy, my cousins and I loved to go to a little pond on our grandparents' property. In the spring we would see tiny tadpoles swimming around near the edges of the pond. We would catch some and put them in a jar to watch for a while before releasing them again. A week or two would go by before we returned to our grandparents' home and continued our adventure.

As we lay on our bellies on the grass by the edge of the water, we noticed our little tadpoles had become big tadpoles. Those strange-looking legs had begun to sprout from their bulbous bodies. By the beginning of summer, we could no longer find our tadpole friends swimming in the shallows. Instead, we found frogs leaping into the water as we approached the pond's edge. The tadpoles had gradually but surely changed. Through the metamorphosis process, they had become like their frog parents who gave them life.

Similarly, the Holy Spirit brings about our metamorphosis, gradually and surely changing us to become more like Jesus, who has given us new birth. The apostle Paul said that change comes "from one degree of glory to another." That phrase could be translated literally "from glory to glory" (2 Corinthians 3:18).

The idea is that the Holy Spirit is changing us *progressively*. He is taking us from one stage of Christlikeness to the next. Sometimes he leads us in a baby step, and sometimes he leads us in a giant step. Either way, he is always bringing us in a sure progression until, as Paul put it, "Christ is formed" in us (Galatians 4:19).

Christians sometimes lose sight of this gradual metamorphosis. We want change *now*. However, don't become impatient or discouraged. Think about how far the Holy Spirit has brought you already. One rough-hewn Christian man put it this way: "I might not be what I *will* be, and I might not be what I *want* to be, but praise God, I'm not what I *used* to be!" Amen.

Encourage your heart with the knowledge that the Holy Spirit is gradually, but surely, changing you to become more and more like Jesus.

But *how* does he do it? Consider a second key word in 2 Corinthians 3:18: *beholding*.

Beholding

The Greek word translated *beholding* in our passage has challenged many translators. In fact, the New Living Translation, for example, translates the word as "reflect." In some Bible passages it communicates the idea of looking at something intently and thoughtfully. In others, the same word carries the idea of mirroring or reflecting back what is shining on it. Both translations are attractive.

We behold, or look intently and thoughtfully, at Jesus Christ as the Holy Spirit removes that veil of spiritual darkness. Then we can see Jesus in all his glory and grace. Paul said that God "has shone in our hearts to give the light of the knowledge of the glory of God in the face of Jesus Christ" (2 Corinthians 4:6).

Some people, including Peter and John, actually saw the glory of Jesus Christ in the flesh. Peter said, "We were eyewitnesses of his majesty" (2 Peter 1:16). And John added his testimony: "We have seen his glory, glory as of the only Son from the Father, full of grace and truth" (John 1:14).

However, we who have not seen Jesus with our physical eyes also have this privilege of looking intently and thoughtfully at Jesus Christ.

1. *The role of Scripture.* As we read the Word of God the Holy Spirit glorifies the Son in our minds and hearts (John 16:14). He shows us the inestimable value of Christ. From cover to cover, the Bible is about Christ. (See Luke 24:27.) So no matter where I am in my daily Bible reading, I like to begin with a brief but sincere prayer: "Holy Spirit, show me Christ today." *He* definitely wants me to see Christ in his Word!

2. *The role of prayer and worship.* As we pray and worship, the Holy Spirit brings us before our Lord Jesus, stirring our minds and hearts so that we stand amazed in his presence. Focusing profoundly on the

glory and grace of Christ can produce the most memorable worship times we will ever enjoy.

3. *The role of suffering.* When we are suffering, the Holy Spirit draws us closer to Christ so that we can contemplate him and find rest for our weary souls.

None of us enjoys suffering. Often our first response is to ask God to take away the pain—of body or soul. But remember that God often brings suffering to remind us that his grace is sufficient. He uses suffering to polish us as his mirrors, cleaning us from whatever might be dulling our reflection of Christ.

As we *behold* Jesus, we also begin to *reflect* him. When Moses went up Mount Sinai, he was exposed to the glory of God. In the presence of the Lord, he began to reflect God's glory. But when he came down from the mountain, Moses didn't even realize that his face was radiant from talking with the Lord.

Christians have a similar privilege. With unveiled hearts, we behold Jesus Christ and see his glory. As we do, we increasingly *reflect* his glory. The Holy Spirit does his work of transformation, and others can progressively see the glory of Jesus in us.

We also increasingly reflect his *character.* His meekness increasingly alters our attitudes and actions. His compassion fills our heart and overflows to others. His joy permeates our daily walk. His love shapes our relationships. Praise the Lord!

Those around us pay attention to this metamorphosis. For example, when the apostles Peter and John were arrested and forced to appear before the religious leaders in Israel, the Sanhedrin members were amazed to observe and hear these unspectacular, uneducated men. These leaders recognized that Peter and John "had been with Jesus" (Acts 4:13).

Many Christians have seen similar reactions from people who knew them before they came to know Christ. Friends, family, and acquaintances often remark on the changes. That's the Holy Spirit's continuing work.

As we increasingly reflect his character, we become moons reflecting the glory of the Son. Our *visible* testimony strengthens our *verbal* testimony for Christ.

The Pure Joy of Being a Mirror

So *who* does Christian maturity look like?" Christian maturity looks like Jesus Christ. We are his mirrors.

To use another analogy, our metamorphosis is like a dimmer switch adjusted brighter and brighter. Maturing Christians want Christlikeness to shine through them in increasing measure. And our reflection of Jesus will grow brighter

- as we spend time with Jesus Christ

- as we spend time thoughtfully gazing at him in his Word—reading it ourselves, meditating on it, and hearing it taught and preached

- as we spend time in prayer, enjoying fellowship with God and asking the Holy Spirit to continue his transforming work in us

- as we spend time engaged in God-honoring, Christ-exalting worship, knowing it's all about him

- as we spend time focusing on God's glory in our suffering. We don't want to waste the suffering he sovereignly brings because suffering is his means of polishing the mirror of our lives so we become better reflectors of his glory.

Like the little boy who wanted to grow up to be a man, our goal is to grow up in the faith to become mature believers in Christ, who reflect his character more and more every day.

Ultimately, we can pray, Lord, change me. Make me more like Jesus. Set me ablaze with the glory of Christ!

Oh! To be like Thee, blessed Redeemer,
This is my constant longing and prayer;
Gladly I'll forfeit all of earth's treasures,
Jesus, Thy perfect likeness to wear.

Oh! to be like Thee, oh! to be like Thee,
Blessed Redeemer, pure as Thou art;
Come in Thy sweetness, come in Thy fullness;
Stamp Thine own image deep on my heart.
—Thomas O. Chisholm

Discussion Questions

THE PRIVILEGE OF WALKING LIKE JESUS

1. What is God's ultimate goal for Christians? Share at least one Bible passage to support your answer.

2. Jerry Bridges, in the foreword of this book uses the word *sanctification* to discuss "a process carried on by the Holy Spirit but involving the intentional response and cooperation of the believer." According to 2 Corinthians 3:17–18, what is the aim of the Holy Spirit in our sanctification?

3. What are some of the processes the Holy Spirit uses in transforming us to become more like Jesus?

4. How can churches be more intentional in encouraging members to become more Christ-focused as a way of life? What role does worship have? The preaching and teaching of the church? The values promoted in the life of the church?

5. Do you have a daily time of reading God's Word and reflecting on Christ? If not, will you make a commitment to begin that discipline of grace in your life? Will you share that commitment with your discussion group or with an accountability partner?

6. Think back over your Christian experience since God saved you. What are some changes the Holy Spirit has worked in your life to make you more like Jesus? Take time and thank him for his transforming work and ask him to help you grow more and more like Jesus.

"Grow in the grace and knowledge of our Lord and Savior Jesus Christ. To him be the glory both now and to the day of eternity. Amen"

—2 Peter 3:18

HOW TO BE RIGHT WITH GOD

As you were reading this book about walking like Jesus, did you sense a growing conviction that you have not yet begun that journey? Reflecting Christ's character takes more than determination to "just do it." The journey of following Christ starts with an inner transformation—a restored relationship between you and your Creator. For each one of us, sin has broken that relationship. But the good news is that God wants to have a personal relationship with us. And he has accomplished everything needed, He explains it all in the Bible:

1. *God has created each of us for his purposes.* We were all born with a God-given job description. The Bible clearly teaches that our Creator God designed you and me to reflect his glory with all we are, with all we have, and with all we do (Isaiah 43:7). He created us to find our greatest joy in seeking his smile and bringing him honor in all things.

2. *Not one of us, on our own, has done—or can do—what God created us for.* Even though God designed us to honor him in all we do, we have selfishly sought our own honor instead. Even though God created us to find our greatest joy in him, we have ignored him and sought our happiness in possessions, power, and pleasure. Isaiah 53:6 makes this painful diagnosis of our condition: "All we like sheep have gone astray; we have turned—every one—to his own way." Jesus Christ was the only exception. And not one other sinless person has existed since sin entered the human race with Adam and Eve's disobedience. "All have sinned and fall short of the glory of God" (Romans 3:23).

3. *God has every right to condemn us to eternal punishment because of our willful rebellion against him.* We have each rebelled against God by seeking our own glory instead of his, and seeking our happiness in things of this world instead of in our Creator. And that is inexcusable. Our rebellion separates us from our loving Creator. It is not as if we didn't know. God has made his identity and power clear through what he has made in creation (Romans 1:19–20). The shameful reality is that we're separated from God because we don't want him in our lives. That is open rebellion against our Creator. The Bible calls that rebellion sin, and sin rightfully earns God's condemnation: "The wages of sin is death" (Romans 6:23). The ultimate death is eternal separation from God in a place of real, conscious torment, known as hell or the lake of fire. The Bible says, "They will suffer the punishment of eternal destruction, away from the presence of the Lord and from the glory of his might" (2 Thessalonians 1:9).

4. *We cannot fix our own terrible dilemma.* God's standard of acceptance is perfection–sinlessness. The Bible teaches us that God is so pure, so holy, that he cannot tolerate sin in the slightest (Habakkuk 1:13). Yet we've all sinned. No amount of good intentions, religious devotion, or benevolent deeds can eradicate our guilt. In fact, even our attempts to justify ourselves are offensive to him. He considers our feeble efforts to make ourselves presentable before his holy throne "like a polluted garment" (Isaiah 64:6). And he holds us accountable. We cannot work our way out of our guilt and into God's good graces. So is our situation hopeless? No.

5. *God himself has provided the only solution to our dreadful predicament.* We *are* guilty. We *are* accountable to God. However, what we would not do and could not do, God did. The Bible tells us, "By sending his own Son in the likeness of sinful flesh and for sin, he condemned sin in the flesh, in order that the righteous requirement of the law might be fulfilled in us" (Romans 8:3–4). Jesus Christ, God's unique Son, came to the earth to keep all of God's laws perfectly. He did for us what we should have done— but did not and could not do by ourselves. He perfectly and con-

sistently glorified God the Father. Then Jesus took on himself the "wages of sin" our rebellion earned. He did this by dying on the cross as a substitute for guilty sinners, such as you and me. "For our sake [God] made him [Jesus] to be sin who knew no sin, so that in him we might become the righteousness of God" (2 Corinthians 5:21, brackets added). As living proof that Jesus' sacrifice on the cross for us satisfied God's holy requirements, God raised Jesus from the dead. Jesus was "raised for our justification" (Romans 4:25).

6. *Christ's sacrifice on the cross opened the door for us to have a right relationship with God*: God graciously calls us to repent of (or turn away from) our sin and all of our attempts to justify ourselves in his eyes. If we ever want to be right with God, he requires us to put all our hope in Jesus Christ alone. "There is salvation in no one else, for there is no other name under heaven given among men by which we must be saved" (Acts 4:12). The Bible also promises, "If you confess with your mouth that Jesus is Lord and believe in your heart that God raised him from the dead, you will be saved. For with the heart one believes and is justified, and with the mouth one confesses and is saved" (Romans 10:9–11).

7. *God wants a relationship with you. How will you respond?* Is God stirring your heart right now? Do you sense your sinfulness before the holy God who made you? Do you want to be right with him? Why don't you talk to God right now? Ask him to forgive your sin and make you his child? Trust in Jesus Christ and what he accomplished on your behalf through his life, death, and resurrection. He will save you. He is gracious beyond your wildest imagination. "To all who did receive him, who believed in his name, he gave the right to become children of God, who were born, not of blood nor of the will of the flesh nor of the will of man, but of God" (John 1:12–13). Isn't that amazing?

8. *God wants you to grow in your relationship with him as you follow—and increasingly reflect—Jesus Christ*: If you have put your trust in Jesus Christ in order to have a right relationship with God, let me encourage you to follow through with some helpful

steps. First, begin reading God's Word on a regular basis. That's how you get to know him better and understand how to live for his glory. The Bible is a big book. Not sure where to start? Try the Gospel of Mark. That's the second book in the New Testament. Second, get into the wonderful habit of talking to God each day in prayer. You don't need fancy, religious words. Just talk to him as your heavenly Father. And third, get plugged into a local church that is faithful in preaching, teaching, and living out the Bible in a way that honors Jesus Christ. Tell some of the leaders of the church what God has been doing in your life and ask for their guidance. Welcome to the family!

ENDNOTES

1   Sinclair B. Ferguson, "Being Like Jesus," *Discipleship Journal* 24 (November 1, 1984): 20.

2   John Stott, *Focus on Christ* (New York: William Collins Publishers, 2019), 95.

3   Dr. Les Carter, *Reflecting the Character of Christ* (Nashville: Thomas Nelson Publishers, 1995), 14.

4   See Paul's illustration in 1 Corinthians 1:26–31, which teaches that accepting "salvation by grace alone" banishes all human pride.

5   Andrew Murray, *Like Christ: Collected Works of Andrew Murray* (Independently published reprint, 2019), 138.

6   J. I. Packer, *Knowing God* (Downers Grove: InterVarsity, 1993), 54.

7   Henry Gariepy, *100 Portraits of Christ* (Colorado Springs: Victor, 1987), 35.

8   Name changed.

9   Frederick Dale Bruner, *Matthew: A Commentary, Revised and Enlarged Edition, 2 vols.* (Grand Rapids: Eerdmans, 2004), 1:505–506.

10 Isaiah 35:5–6; 26:19; 61:1–3.

11 William Garden Blaikie, *Glimpses of the Inner Life of Christ* (Independently published reprint, 2017), 60.

12 Murray, *Like Christ,* 87.

13 See John 8:46; 2 Corinthians 5:21; Hebrews 4:15; 1 Peter 1:19; 1 John 3:5.

14 Jerry Bridges, *Trusting God* (Colorado Springs: NavPress, 1988), 200.

15 See 2 Corinthians 11:23–29 for more about the sufferings Paul endured during his life of ministry.

16 John Bunyan, *The Whole Works of John Bunyan, Volume III* (Grand Rapids: Baker, 1977 reprint), 386.

17 Charles Spurgeon, *Morning and Evening*, (Ross-shire, Scotland: Christian Focus Publications Ltd., 1997 reprint), October 24, evening.

18 James S. Stewart, *The Life and Teaching of Jesus Christ* (New York: Abingdon Press, 2000 reprint), 98.

19 Blaikie, *Glimpses,* 113.

20 John A. Broadus, *Jesus of Nazareth* (CreateSpace, 2018), 13–14.

21 J. Oswald Sanders, *The Incomparable Christ* (Chicago: Moody, 2009), 189.

22 Charles Spurgeon, *The Metropolitan Tabernacle Pulpit, Vol. 30* (Pasadena, TX: Pilgrim Publications, 1973 reprint), 136.

23 Murray, *Like Christ,* 133.

24 Charles Edward Jefferson, *The Character of Jesus* (Forgotten Books, 2008), 247.

25 Robert Law, *The Emotions of Jesus* (Edinburgh: T. & T. Clark, 1915), 5.

26 Blaikie, *Glimpses*, 109.

27 Elton Trueblood, *The Humor of Jesus* (New York: Harper & Row, 1964), 32.

28 Octavius Winslow, *The Sympathy of Christ* (Harrisonburg, VA: Sprinkle Publications, 1994), 216.

29 John Piper, *The Passion of Jesus Christ* (Wheaton: Crossway, 2004), 30–31.

30 D. A. Carson, *The Farewell Discourse and Final Prayer of Jesus* (Grand Rapids: Baker, 1980), 103.

31 Names changed.

32 Stott, *Focus*, 153.